LITTLE

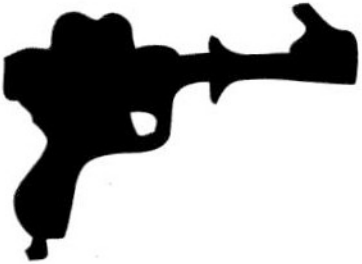

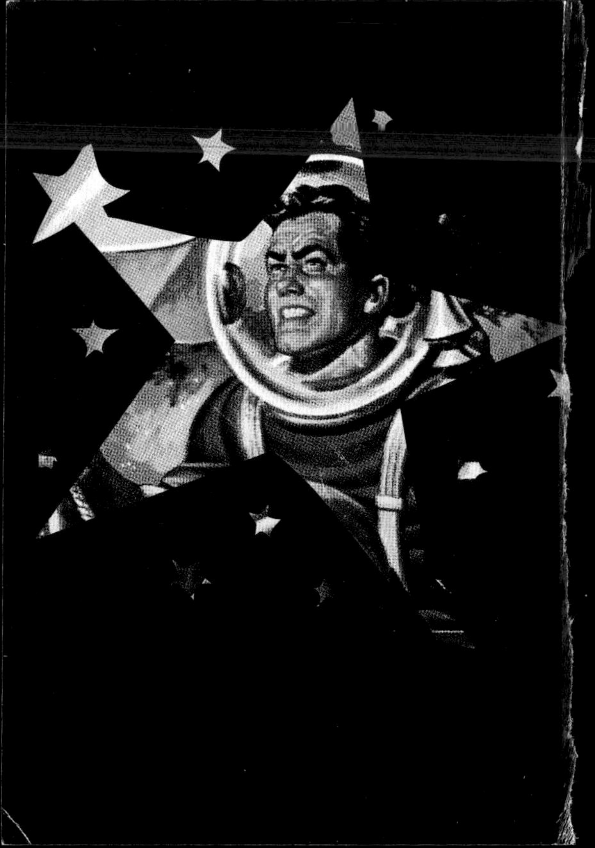

LITTLE BOOK OF VINTAGE

Sci-Fi

TIM PILCHER

ILEX

LITTLE BOOK OF VINTAGE: SCI-FI

First published in the UK, US, and Canada
in 2012 by
I L E X
210 High Street
Lewes
East Sussex BN7 2NS
www.ilex-press.com

Publisher: Alastair Campbell
Creative Director: James Hollywell
Managing Editor: Nick Jones
Senior Editor: Ellie Wilson
Commissioning Editor: Tim Pilcher
Art Director: Julie Weir
Designer: Simon Goggin

British Library Cataloguing-in-Publication Data
A catalogue record for this book is available from the British Library.

ISBN: 978-1-908150-39-4

Printed and bound in China

Colour Origination by Ivy Press Reprographics

10 9 8 7 6 5 4 3 2

Alienator font courtesy of Cosmonaut Fonts
Raygun font courtesy of Pushplayround

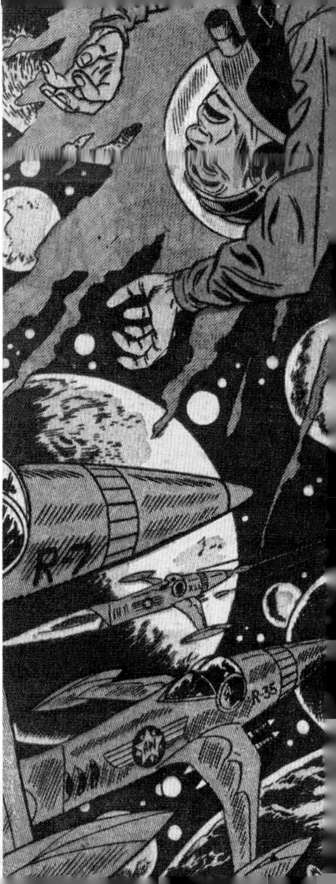
R-35

Contents

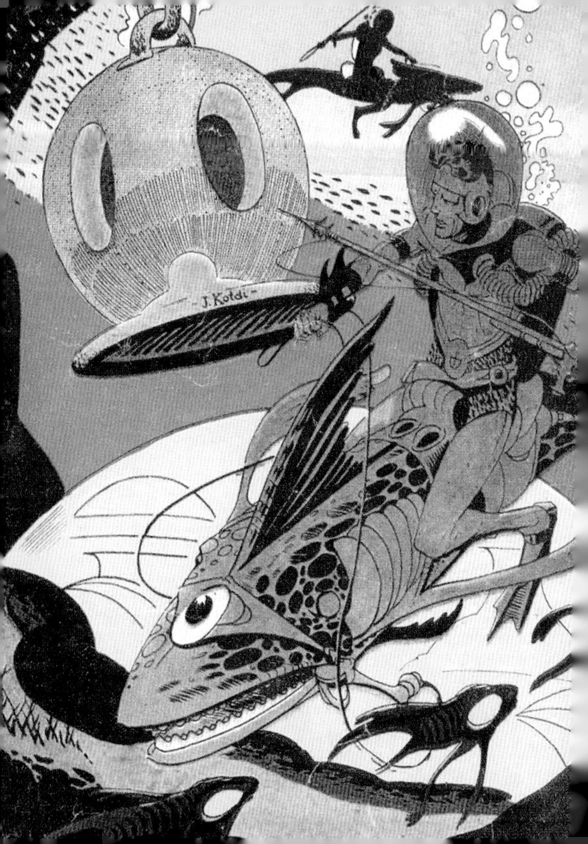
-J. Koldi-

Introduction

The cover of *Adventures into the Unknown #46* (August, 1953) asked, "Who knows what strange and terrible lands may lay beyond man's knowledge . . . What dread creatures may lie in wait for the unwary . . . " It was a question that practically every American sci-fi comic of the Fifties tried to answer.

The first US science fiction comic strips to blast off into the unknown appeared on the pages of the national newspapers, with strips such as Philip Nowlan, John F. Dille, and artist Dick Calkins' *Buck Rogers* (1929) and Alex Raymond's *Flash Gordon* (1934). *Planet Comics* (1940) was one of the earliest comic books completely devoted to the genre and featured classic characters like Mysta of the Moon; Star Pirate–"The Robin Hood of the space lanes;" Auro, Lord of Jupiter; and Spurt Hammond, "Human defender of the Planet Venus." Ironically, the comic folded in 1953, just as the US/Russian "Space Race" heralded a huge explosion of science fiction and space-related stories in American popular culture, and their upswing in sci-fi comic books reflected this.

The *Tom Corbett, Space Cadet* (published by Dell) and *Space Patrol* (Ziff-Davis) comics both launched in 1952 and were spin-offs from popular sci-fi TV series. However, the latter only made it to two issues before being left adrift in space. Connecticut-based publisher Charlton's huge range of space-based titles included *Space Adventures* (1952), *Out of This World* (1956), *Mysteries of Unexplored Worlds* (1956), and *Outer Space* (1958). All featured fantastically accomplished art by comics legend–and co-creator of *Spider-Man*–Steve Ditko. Charlton also went down the cross-genre path with *Space War* (1959) and the slightly more esoteric *Space Western Comics* (1952) "featuring Spurs Jackson and his Space Vigilantes!"

Other classic titles included *Captain Science* (1950), *Alarming Tales* (1957), *Fantastic Worlds* (1952), and ACG's *Operation Peril* (1950), which was a mixed bag of heavily—but not exclusively—science-fiction-based adventures. Avon's *Strange Worlds* (1950) featured *Kenton of the Star Patrol* by artist Wally Wood. Wood became the most renowned of the Fifties sci-fi comic artists and convinced EC publisher William Gaines to launch his own science fiction comics, *Weird Science* and *Weird Fantasy*, in 1950. However, EC's sci-fi titles never took off in the same way as their horror and crime ones, despite the same creative teams working on them. Consequently, the two titles were merged into *Weird Science Fantasy* in 1954. The title was changed to *Incredible Science Fiction* the following year in order to comply with the new Comics Code Authority's ruling that the word "Weird" could no longer be used in a title. It only limped on for another four issues before finally running out of steam.

With television becoming increasingly popular and space travel becoming science fact, it was inevitable that science fiction comics' popularity would drastically wane by the end of the Fifties. As the "Weird, Mysterious" and "Spine-Tingling" *Adventures into the Unknown* #88 (September, 1957) revealed, "There are many ways of bridging time—This way—Or through the most astounding use of memory you've ever encountered!" So put on your space helmet, grab your sonic blaster, and strap yourself into the time machine. We're about to step back into yesteryear's sci-fi comics, today!

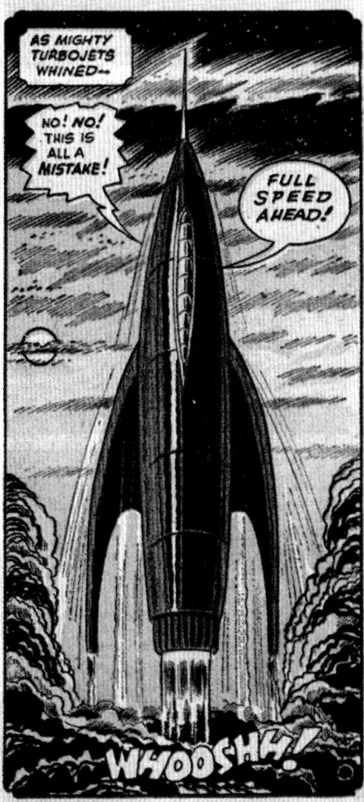
AS MIGHTY TURBOJETS WHINED--
NO! NO! THIS IS ALL A MISTAKE!
FULL SPEED AHEAD!
WHOOSHH!

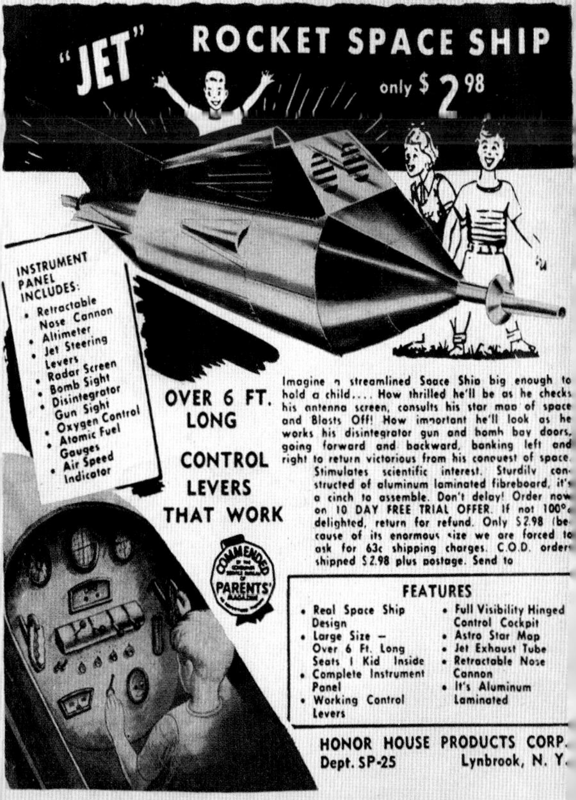
"JET" ROCKET SPACE SHIP
only $2.98
INSTRUMENT PANEL INCLUDES:
• Retractable Nose Cannon
• Altimeter
• Jet Steering Levers
• Radar Screen
• Bomb Sight
• Disintegrator Gun Sight
• Oxygen Control
• Atomic Fuel Gauges
• Air Speed Indicator
OVER 6 FT. LONG
CONTROL LEVERS THAT WORK
Imagine a streamlined Space Ship big enough to hold a child.... How thrilled he'll be as he checks his antenna screen, consults his star map of space and Blasts Off! How important he'll look as he works his disintegrator gun and bomb bay doors, going forward and backward, banking left and right to return victorious from his conquest of space. Stimulates scientific interest. Sturdily constructed of aluminum laminated fibreboard, it's a cinch to assemble. Don't delay! Order now on 10 DAY FREE TRIAL OFFER. If not 100% delighted, return for refund. Only $2.98 (because of its enormous size we are forced to ask for 63c shipping charges. C.O.D. orders shipped $2.98 plus postage. Send to
COMMENDED PARENTS' MAGAZINE
FEATURES
• Real Space Ship Design
• Large Size — Over 6 Ft. Long Seats 1 Kid Inside
• Complete Instrument Panel
• Working Control Levers
• Full Visibility Hinged Control Cockpit
• Astro Star Map
• Jet Exhaust Tube
• Retractable Nose Cannon
• It's Aluminum Laminated
HONOR HOUSE PRODUCTS CORP.
Dept. SP-25
Lynbrook, N. Y.

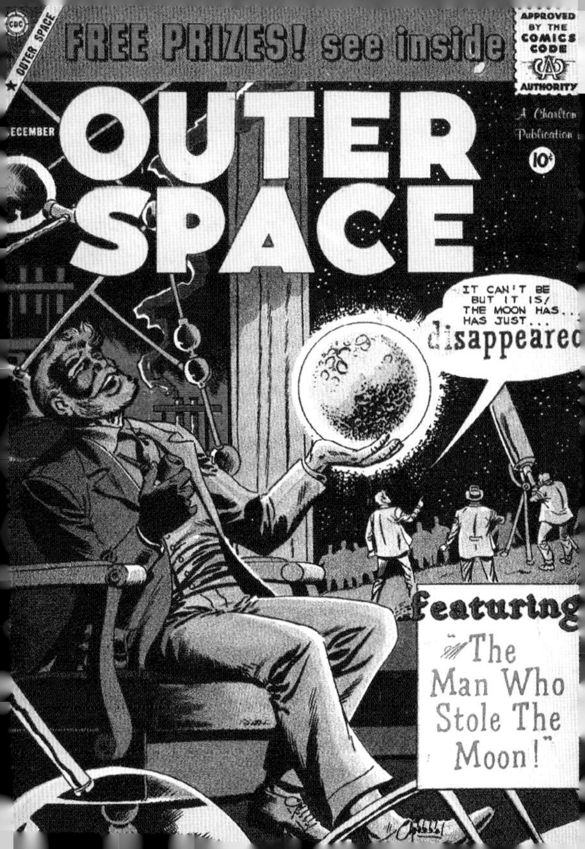
CDC
OUTER SPACE
FREE PRIZES! see inside
APPROVED BY THE COMICS CODE AUTHORITY
DECEMBER
OUTER SPACE
A Charlton Publication
10¢
IT CAN'T BE BUT IT IS/ THE MOON HAS... HAS JUST... disappeared
featuring
"The Man Who Stole The Moon!"

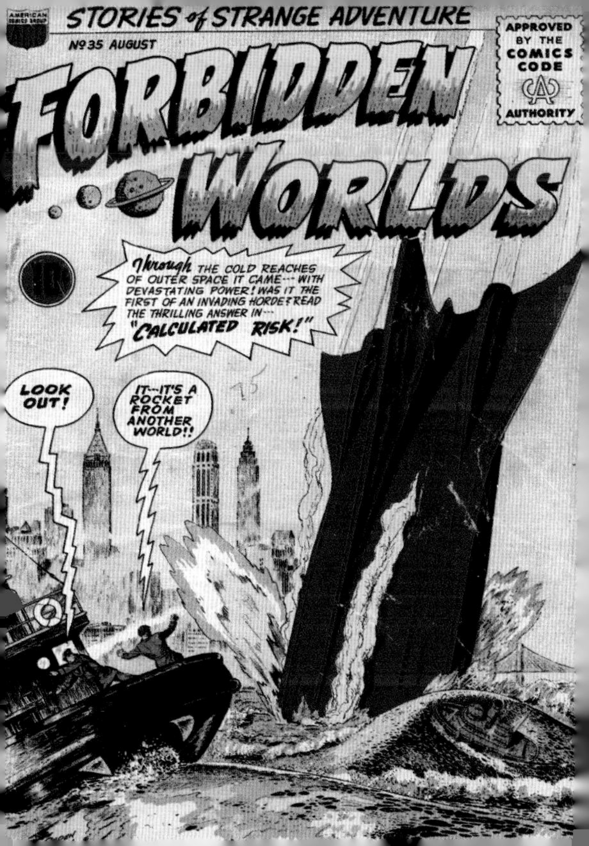
AMERICAN COMICS GROUP
STORIES of STRANGE ADVENTURE
№35 AUGUST
FORBIDDEN WORLDS
APPROVED BY THE COMICS CODE AUTHORITY
Through THE COLD REACHES OF OUTER SPACE IT CAME--- WITH DEVASTATING POWER! WAS IT THE FIRST OF AN INVADING HORDE? READ THE THRILLING ANSWER IN--- "CALCULATED RISK!"
LOOK OUT!
IT--IT'S A ROCKET FROM ANOTHER WORLD!!

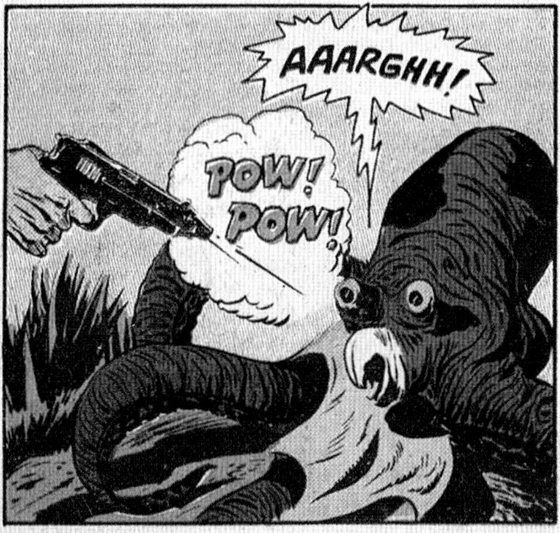
AAARGHH!
POW! POW!

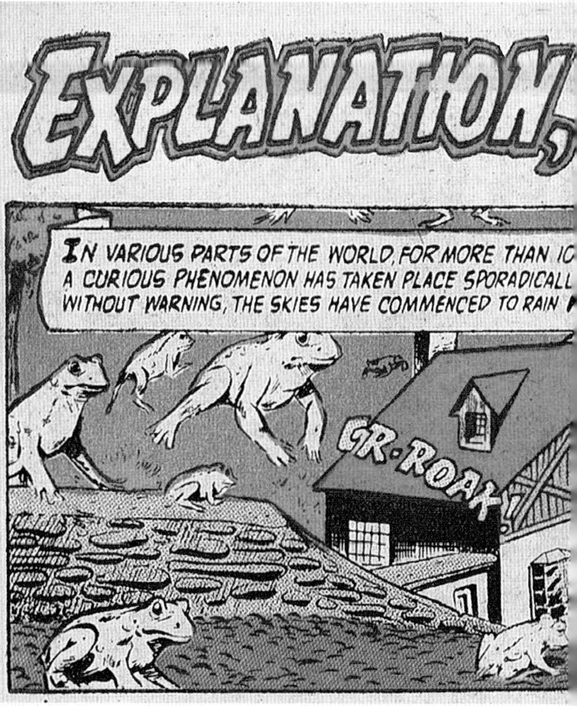
EXPLANATION,
IN VARIOUS PARTS OF THE WORLD, FOR MORE THAN IC
A CURIOUS PHENOMENON HAS TAKEN PLACE SPORADICALL
WITHOUT WARNING, THE SKIES HAVE COMMENCED TO RAIN
GR-ROAK!

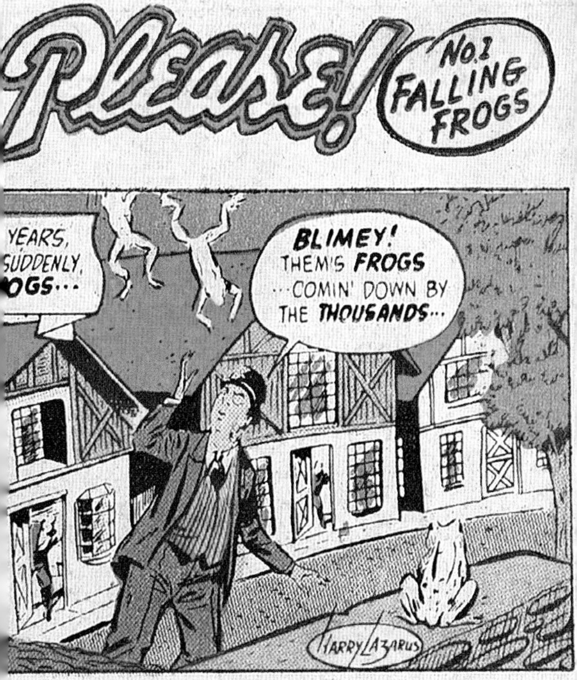
PLEASE!
No.1 FALLING FROGS
YEARS,
SUDDENLY,
OGS...
BLIMEY! THEM'S FROGS ...COMIN' DOWN BY THE THOUSANDS...
HARRY LAZARUS

A FAMILIAR EXPLANATION HAS USUALLY FOLLOWED...
OBVIOUSLY SOME WHIRLWIND SCOOPED UP A LAKE OR POND AND DEPOSITED THE FROGS SOME DISTANCE AWAY! THE CIRCUMSTANCE MAY BE UNUSUAL, BUT PERFECTLY EXPLICABLE!

THE ONLY TROUBLE IS, MANY SCIENTISTS REFUSE TO ACCEPT THE EXPLANATION...
RIDICULOUS! NOBODY HAS REPORTED LOSING A LAKE! FURTHERMORE, A THOROUGH INVESTIGATION HAS FAILED TO SHOW ANY REPORT OF ANY WHIRLWIND WITHIN THOUSANDS OF MILES!

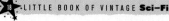

AS ALREADY STATED, THE EVENT HAS TAKEN PLACE ALMOST EVERYWHERE, AND CAREFUL STUDIES ALWAYS REVEAL THE SAME BAFFLING MYSTERIES...

IF A **WHIRLWIND** IS RESPONSIBLE, WHY DO ONLY **FROGS** COME DOWN? WHY NOT WATER PLANTS, FISHES, TURTLES...?

YES, AND WHY ARE THEY ALWAYS **YOUNG** FROGS... JUST A FEW MONTHS OF AGE? AND WHY ARE THEY ALWAYS UNUSUALLY **WHITE?**

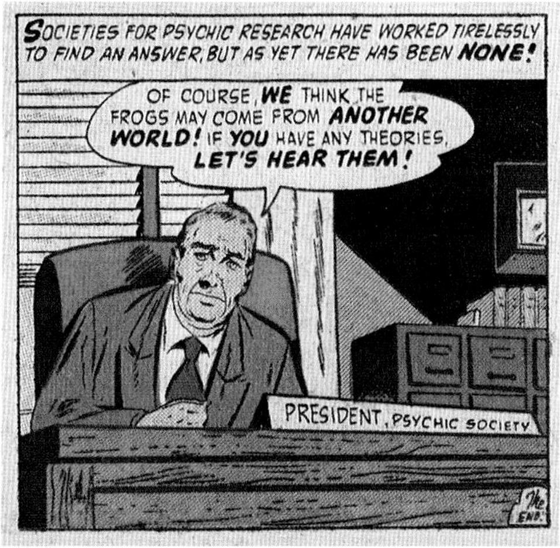
SOCIETIES FOR PSYCHIC RESEARCH HAVE WORKED TIRELESSLY TO FIND AN ANSWER, BUT AS YET THERE HAS BEEN NONE!
OF COURSE, WE THINK THE FROGS MAY COME FROM ANOTHER WORLD! IF YOU HAVE ANY THEORIES, LET'S HEAR THEM!
PRESIDENT, PSYCHIC SOCIETY

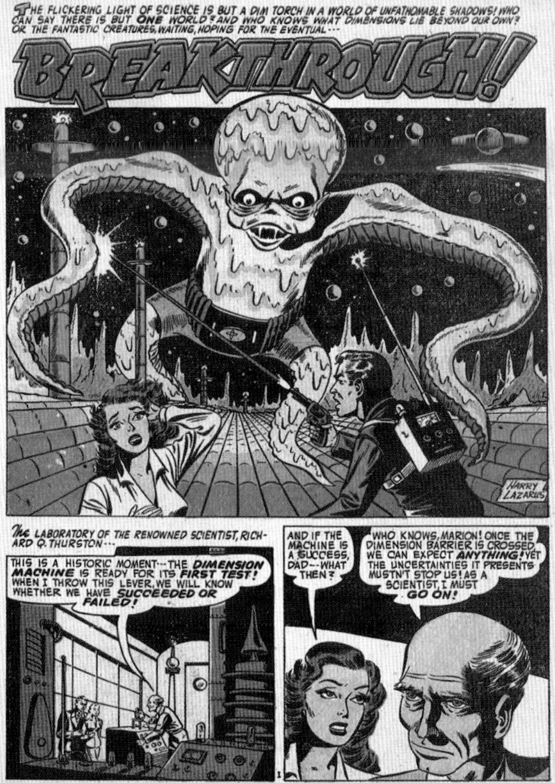
THE FLICKERING LIGHT OF SCIENCE IS BUT A DIM TORCH IN A WORLD OF UNFATHOMABLE SHADOWS! WHO CAN SAY THERE IS BUT ONE WORLD? AND WHO KNOWS WHAT DIMENSIONS LIE BEYOND OUR OWN? OR THE FANTASTIC CREATURES, WAITING, HOPING FOR THE EVENTUAL ---
BREAKTHROUGH!
HARRY LAZARUS
THE LABORATORY OF THE RENOWNED SCIENTIST, RICHARD Q. THURSTON ---
THIS IS A HISTORIC MOMENT -- THE DIMENSION MACHINE IS READY FOR ITS FIRST TEST! WHEN I THROW THIS LEVER, WE WILL KNOW WHETHER WE HAVE SUCCEEDED OR FAILED!
AND IF THE MACHINE IS A SUCCESS, DAD -- WHAT THEN?
WHO KNOWS, MARION! ONCE THE DIMENSION BARRIER IS CROSSED WE CAN EXPECT ANYTHING! YET THE UNCERTAINTIES IT PRESENTS MUSTN'T STOP US! AS A SCIENTIST, I MUST GO ON!
1

ADVENTURES INTO THE UNKNOWN, published monthly and copyright, 1953, by Best Syndicated Features, Inc., 420 DeSoto Avenue, St. Louis 7, Missouri. Editorial offices, 45 West 45 Street, New York 36, N. Y. Richard E. Hughes, Editor; Frederick H. Iger, Business Manager. Subscription (12 issues), $1.20; single copies, $0.10; foreign postage extra. All characters are fictitious and use of any real names is coincidental. For advertising information, address American Comics Group, 45 West 45 Street, New York 36, N. Y. Re-entered as second class matter at the Post Office at St. Louis, Missouri. No. 46, August, 1953. Printed in U.S.A.

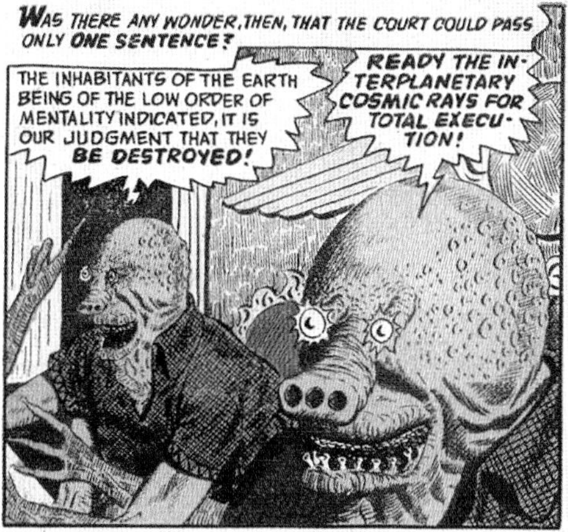
WAS THERE ANY WONDER, THEN, THAT THE COURT COULD PASS ONLY ONE SENTENCE?
THE INHABITANTS OF THE EARTH BEING OF THE LOW ORDER OF MENTALITY INDICATED, IT IS OUR JUDGMENT THAT THEY BE DESTROYED!
READY THE INTERPLANETARY COSMIC RAYS FOR TOTAL EXECUTION!

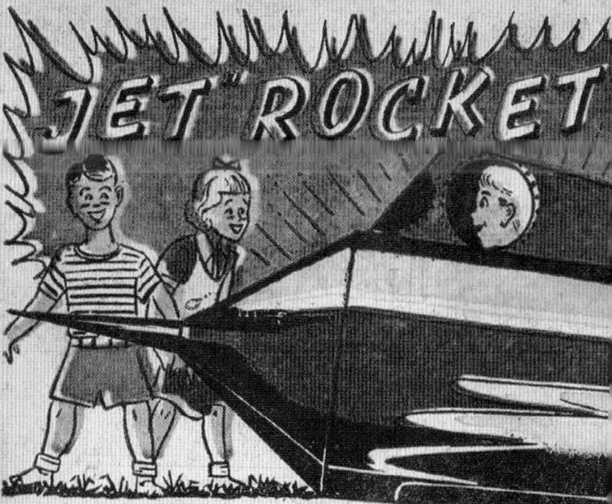
"JET" ROCKET

THE MOST SENSATIONAL TOY IN AMERICA

FEATURES

- Real Space Ship Design
- Sturdy Interlocked Construction
- Made of High Strength 3 ply Fibreboard
- Large Size — Over 7 feet Long. Large enough for 2 space cadets
- Complete Instrument Panel
- 2 Disintegrator Guns
- Full Visibility Hinged Control Cockpit
- Astro-star map
- 2 Steering Planes
- Elevator and Rudder
- Aluminum Jet Exhaust Tube

It's Gigantic — Over 7 Feet Long   Control levers tha

For you — a real streamlined Space Ship big enough to hold you and a pal on trips through space. It's complete with all the newest scientific advances of flights of the future. There's no more make-believe, no more pretending with small models. This is really it! You are pilot, captain, and gunner — your friend can be observer and navigator.

Imagine all this!

There you are giving orders as captain of your own sleek, st lined beauty. You check your radar antenna screen for all You test all radio instruments and equipment. You clos hinged cockpit cover and check your Star Map of space. with all your jet and rocket flying equipment in action BLAST OFF! You set your course, steering with the direc jets at the stern which are controlled by separate thrott your fingertips. Your forward disintegrator guns go into a Your fully-equipped radar instrument panel shows the t You release your load of powerful nuclear bombs and bul You return home victoriously, set your reversing mechanis you're in for a quick landing. This is just an idea of a wonderful things you can do with your sensational new Ship. Sturdily constructed of 3-ply fibreboard, it will brin more fun and adventure than you've ever known. Ea assemble

Only

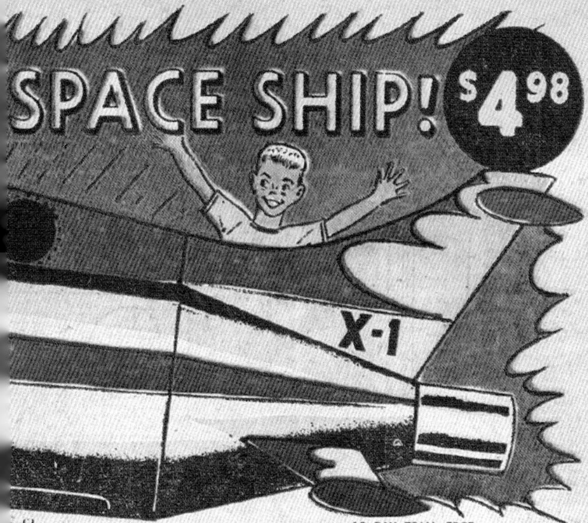
SPACE SHIP!
$4.98
X-1

ɔrk!

10 DAY TRIAL FREE

Don't delay! Order now! We are so sure you will be thrilled as never before, we offer you a full 10-Day Free Trial under our ironclad MONEY BACK GUARANTEE plan. Because of its gigantic size, we are forced to ask for 63¢ postage charges.

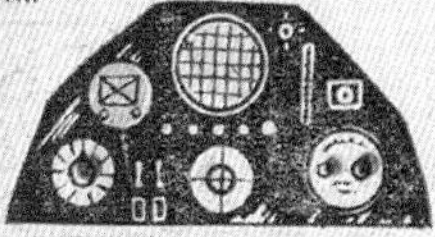

INSTRUMENT PANEL INCLUDES

- ALTIMETER
- JET STEERING LEVERS
- JET REVERSING LEVER
- RADAR SCREEN
- RADIO INSTRUMENTS
- BOMB SIGHT
- DISINTEGRATOR GUN SIGHT
- BOMB BAY DOOR CONTROL
- HOOD LATCH CONTROL
- OXYGEN CONTROL
- ATOMIC FUEL GAUGES
- AIR SPEED INDICATOR
- BLAST OFF SIGNAL BUTTON

MONEY BACK GUARANTEE

Honor House Products Corp. Dept. A-169
35 Wilbur St., Lynbrook, N. Y.

Rush my jet "Rocket" Space Ship on 10 Day Free Trial for only $4.98. If I am not completely delighted I may return it for prompt refund of full purchase price.

☐ Send C.O.D. I'll pay postman $4.98 plus postage.

☐ I enclose $4.98 plus 63¢ postage and handling charge for my Space Ship. Same Money Back Guarantee.

NAME ____________________

ADDRESS ____________________

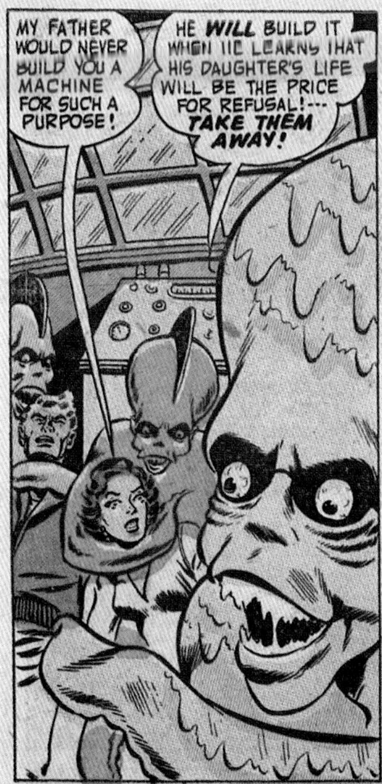
MY FATHER WOULD NEVER BUILD YOU A MACHINE FOR SUCH A PURPOSE!
HE WILL BUILD IT WHEN HE LEARNS THAT HIS DAUGHTER'S LIFE WILL BE THE PRICE FOR REFUSAL!--- TAKE THEM AWAY!

The INHUMAN HUMANS

I T . . . IT's fantastic . . . unbelievable!" Charles Waverly muttered, wiping the cold sweat away from his forehead. "But it's all here, in black and white—in Dr. Jorgensen's secret files! And it all fits in—now I'm beginning to understand it all . . ."

Yes, the pieces were beginning to fit together in Charles Waverly's mind. Now he knew the reason why Dr. Jorgensen's biological laboratory was deep in the Michigan Northwoods . . . why Jorgie never allowed anyone but himself to enter the vaulted, inner labs . . . why Charles and all the other chemists, physiologists and geneticists all had hazy memories of their past.

Jorgie had told them that when he first hired them fresh from their universities, they had willingly subjected themselves to a special injection that stepped up their intelligence more than tenfold—but that had the unfortunate effect of blotting out all non-scientific memories from infancy on. It had all seemed plausible to them, and Jorgie had gotten them all to admit that their memories were but a minor sacrifice for the great scientific cause they were working on. No one had ever complained—they had all worked ten and twelve hours a day in the labs, aiding Jorgie's great researches into the causes and origins of life itself.

But yesterday had brought the first real change in their routinized lives in years—for their beloved Jorgie had died suddenly of a heart attack. With his dying words, he had told Charles Waverly to take charge of all the labs—and with his dying effort, he had given him the keys to all the secret files and vaults.

Charles had known that Jorgie would have wanted him to plunge into his new duties immediately, without wasting any time in mourning—and so only an hour ago, Charles had started going through the files which no eyes but Jorgie's had ever seen before. And what he had found was fantastic . . . unbelievable . . .

Thirty years ago, the files revealed, Dr. Jorgensen had discovered the secret of creating protoplasm—of creating life! With his vast knowledge, he had started electronic breeders and incubators for the production of artificial humans—and had been successful! But Jorgie had been afraid to inform the world of his discoveries until he could be sure his humans would not grow into freaks and monstrosities. And then, when his specimens had matured normally in the incubators, he had subjected their unconscious minds to almost all the scientific lore at his command—and had removed them from the machines to see if they would act and think as humans. After subjecting them to hundreds of psychological tests, he had found that they were normal in all respects—except that they had a strange pathological need to feel that they were all average normal humans, born of human parents.

And because Jorgie feared his creations would go insane if he told them they weren't really human, he had never revealed his secret to them or to the world.

With mounting horror, Charles Waverly glanced down the list of names of artificial humans—Harold Arlen—John Crawford—Jules Hyatt—Leonard Marx—all of them his colleagues and friends—and all of them horribly inhuman! A sudden catastrophic thought hit Charles—what if he—? But no—he, Charles Waverly, had to be human—or else Jorgie would never have put him in charge of the labs! Realizing that he could never bear being a . . . an artificial, inhuman thing, Charles breathed a sigh of relief and went on reading the names of the specimens. Donald Robinson . . . Leo Thomas . . . Charles Waverly!

Instantly, it seemed as if a raging inferno had consumed Charles Waverly's brain, and with the cunning born of madness, he suddenly knew just how he would blow up the labs and all their inhuman creations.

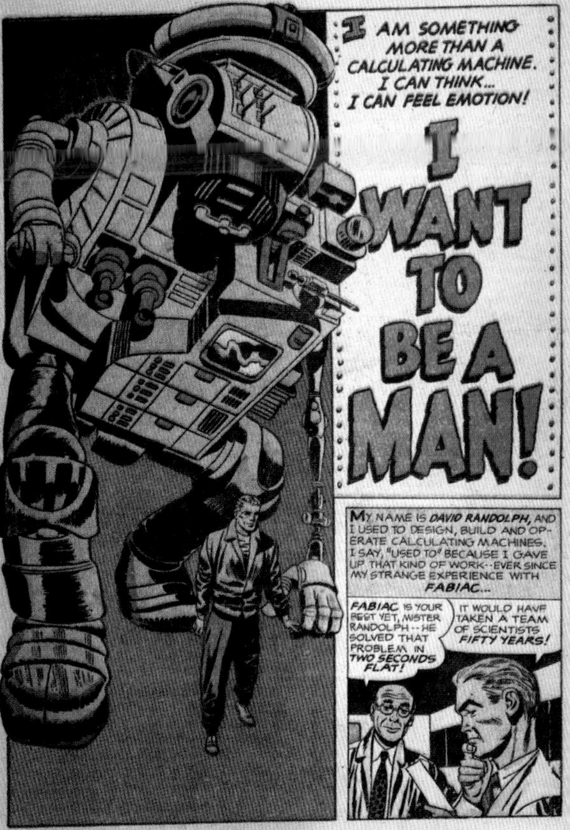
I AM SOMETHING MORE THAN A CALCULATING MACHINE. I CAN THINK... I CAN FEEL EMOTION!
I WANT TO BE A MAN!
MY NAME IS DAVID RANDOLPH, AND I USED TO DESIGN, BUILD AND OPERATE CALCULATING MACHINES. I SAY, "USED TO" BECAUSE I GAVE UP THAT KIND OF WORK--EVER SINCE MY STRANGE EXPERIENCE WITH FABIAC...
FABIAC IS YOUR BEST YET, MISTER RANDOLPH--HE SOLVED THAT PROBLEM IN TWO SECONDS FLAT!
IT WOULD HAVE TAKEN A TEAM OF SCIENTISTS FIFTY YEARS!

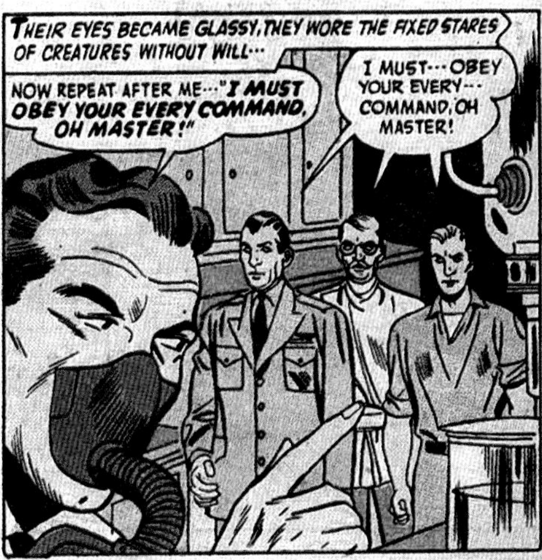
THEIR EYES BECAME GLASSY, THEY WORE THE FIXED STARES OF CREATURES WITHOUT WILL...
NOW REPEAT AFTER ME..."I MUST OBEY YOUR EVERY COMMAND, OH MASTER!"
I MUST... OBEY YOUR EVERY... COMMAND, OH MASTER!

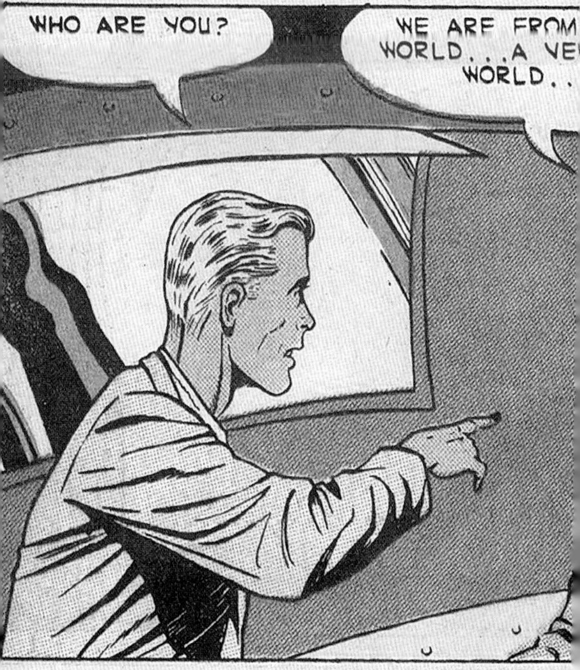
WHO ARE YOU?
WE ARE FROM WORLD...A VE WORLD..

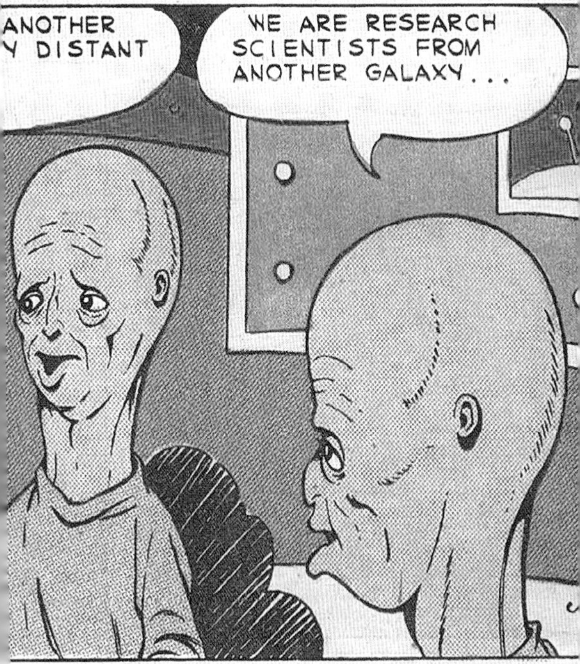
ANOTHER
Y DISTANT
WE ARE RESEARCH SCIENTISTS FROM ANOTHER GALAXY...

CAPTAIN STRONG CALLING THE SPACE CADETS! CAPTAIN STRONG CALLING THE SPACE CADETS!

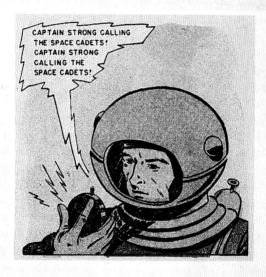

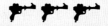

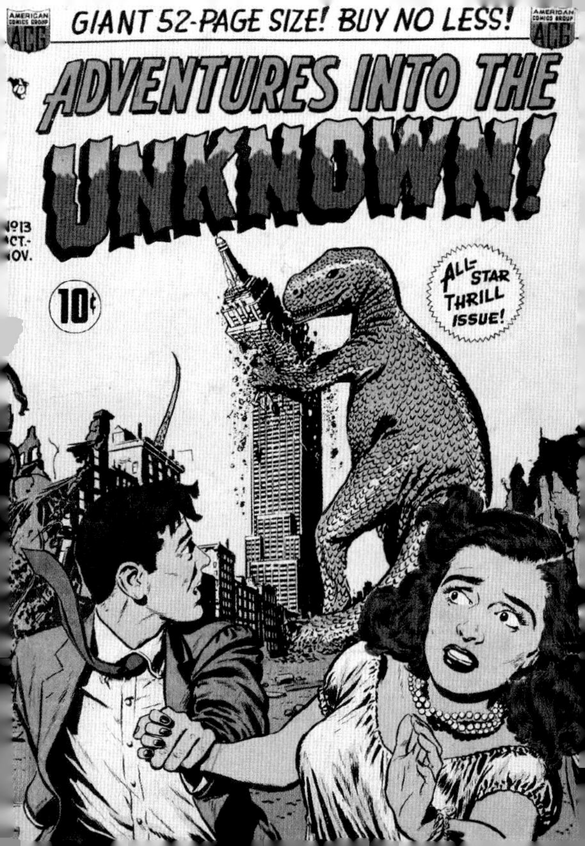

AMERICAN COMICS GROUP ACG
GIANT 52-PAGE SIZE! BUY NO LESS!
AMERICAN COMICS GROUP ACG
ADVENTURES INTO THE UNKNOWN!
Nº13
CT.-
OV.
10¢
ALL-STAR THRILL ISSUE!

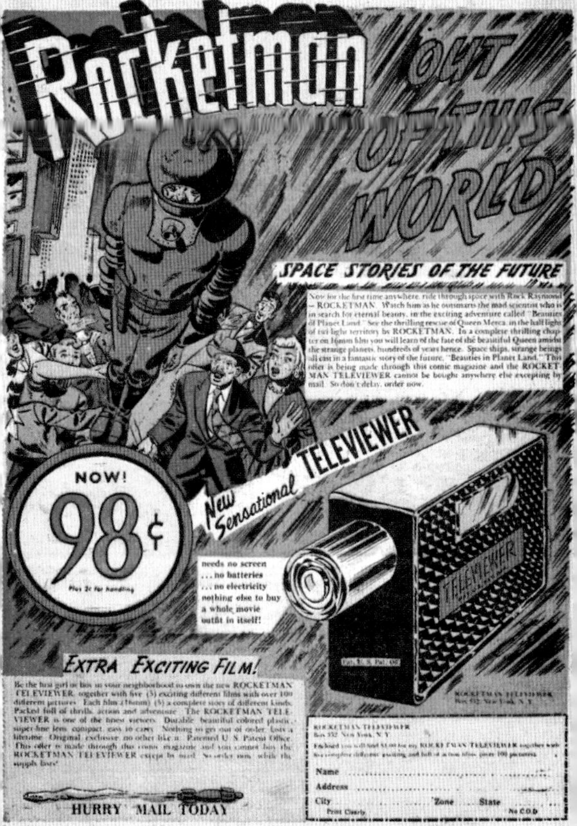

Rocketman
OUT OF THIS WORLD
SPACE STORIES OF THE FUTURE
Now for the first time anywhere, ride through space with Rock Raymond — ROCKETMAN. Watch him as he outsmarts the mad scientist who is in search for eternal beauty, in the exciting adventure called "Beauties of Planet Land." See the thrilling rescue of Queen Merca, in the half light of twi-light territory by ROCKETMAN. In a complete thrilling chapter on 16mm film you will learn of the fate of the beautiful Queen amidst the strange planets, hundreds of years hence. Space ships, strange beings all cast in a fantastic story of the future, "Beauties in Planet Land." This offer is being made through this comic magazine and the ROCKETMAN TELEVIEWER cannot be bought anywhere else excepting by mail. So don't delay, order now.
New Sensational TELEVIEWER
NOW!
98¢
needs no screen
... no batteries
... no electricity
nothing else to buy
a whole movie outfit in itself!
TELEVIEWER
EXTRA EXCITING FILM!
Name
Address
City
Zone
State
Print Clearly
No C.O.D.
HURRY MAIL TODAY

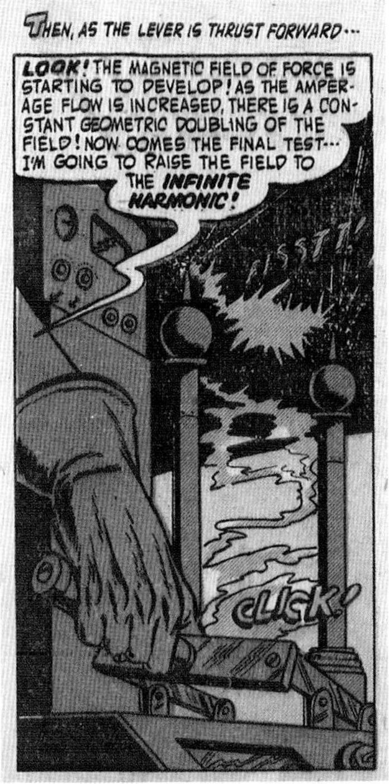
THEN, AS THE LEVER IS THRUST FORWARD...
LOOK! THE MAGNETIC FIELD OF FORCE IS STARTING TO DEVELOP! AS THE AMPERAGE FLOW IS INCREASED, THERE IS A CONSTANT GEOMETRIC DOUBLING OF THE FIELD! NOW COMES THE FINAL TEST... I'M GOING TO RAISE THE FIELD TO THE INFINITE HARMONIC!
FISSTT!
CLICK!

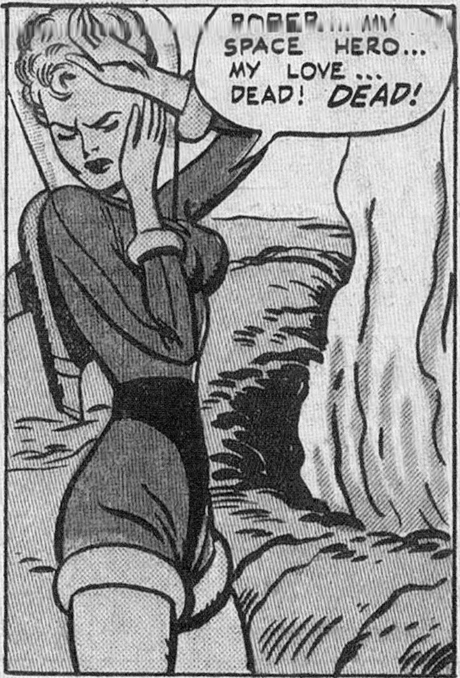
SPACE HERO...
MY LOVE ...
DEAD! *DEAD!*

MANY MONUMENTAL STRUCTURES HAVE RISEN ON EARTH--THE PYRAMIDS, THE GREAT WALL OF CHINA, THE MOUNT RUSHMORE STONE FACES...BUT NONE OF THESE EARTHLY WONDERS CAN COMPARE WITH THE GREAT STONE FACE OF SPACE, CARVED OUT OF HALF A WORLD! GIGANTIC, FANTASTIC, MYSTERIOUS...WHAT ANSWER IS THERE TO THE RIDDLE OF...

the SPACE LORELEI

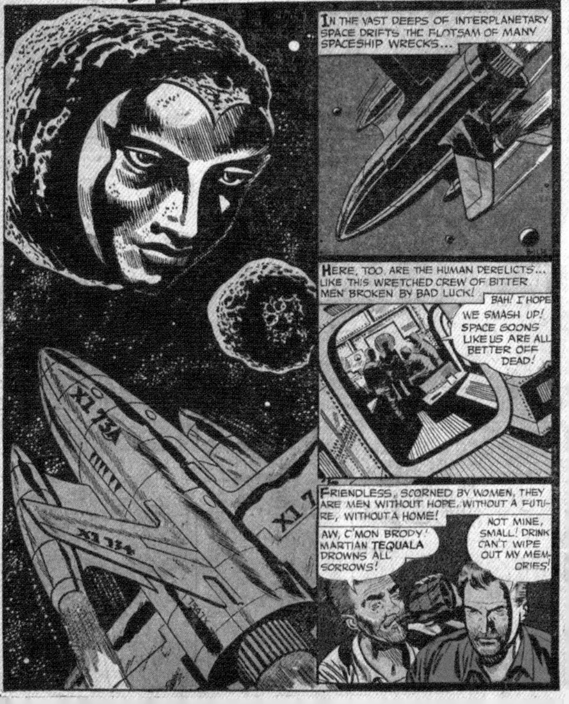
IN THE VAST DEEPS OF INTERPLANETARY SPACE DRIFTS THE FLOTSAM OF MANY SPACESHIP WRECKS...
HERE, TOO ARE THE HUMAN DERELICTS...LIKE THIS WRETCHED CREW OF BITTER MEN BROKEN BY BAD LUCK!
BAH! I HOPE WE SMASH UP! SPACE GOONS LIKE US ARE ALL BETTER OFF DEAD!
FRIENDLESS, SCORNED BY WOMEN, THEY ARE MEN WITHOUT HOPE, WITHOUT A FUTURE, WITHOUT A HOME!
AW, C'MON BRODY! MARTIAN TEQUALA DROWNS ALL SORROWS!
NOT MINE, SMALL! DRINK CAN'T WIPE OUT MY MEMORIES!

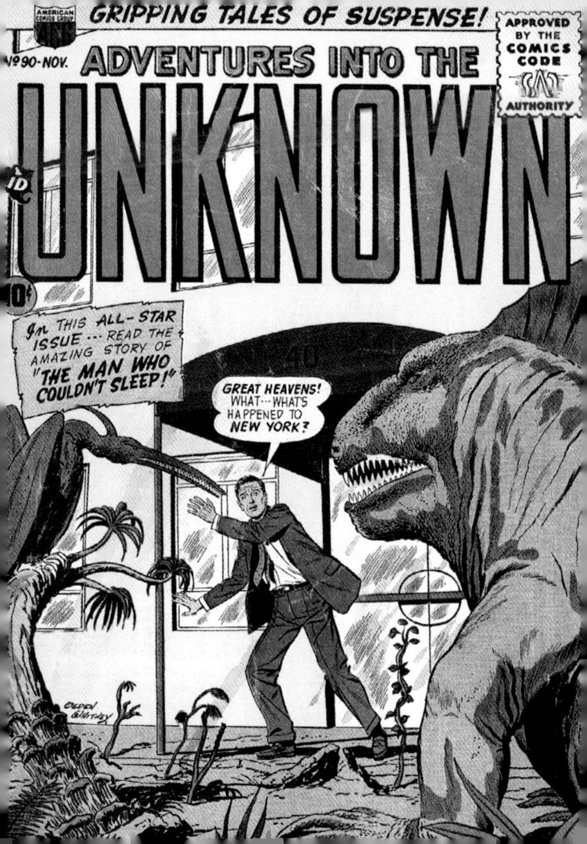

AMERICAN COMICS GROUP
GRIPPING TALES OF SUSPENSE!
APPROVED BY THE COMICS CODE AUTHORITY
№90-NOV.
ADVENTURES INTO THE
UNKNOWN
10¢
In THIS ALL-STAR ISSUE --- READ THE AMAZING STORY OF "THE MAN WHO COULDN'T SLEEP!"
GREAT HEAVENS! WHAT--- WHAT'S HAPPENED TO NEW YORK?
OGDEN WHITNEY

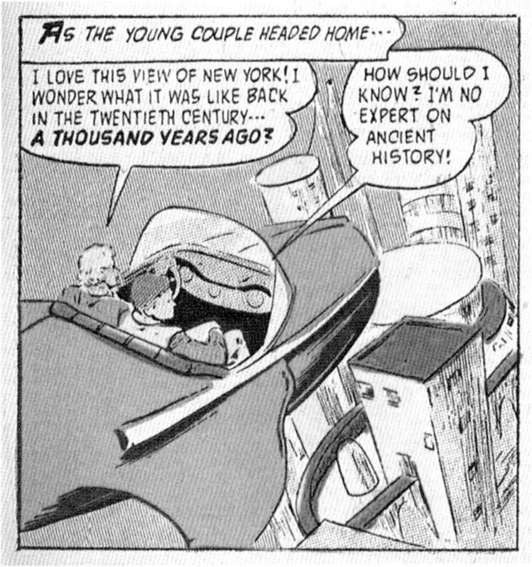
AS THE YOUNG COUPLE HEADED HOME…
I LOVE THIS VIEW OF NEW YORK! I WONDER WHAT IT WAS LIKE BACK IN THE TWENTIETH CENTURY… A THOUSAND YEARS AGO?
HOW SHOULD I KNOW? I'M NO EXPERT ON ANCIENT HISTORY!

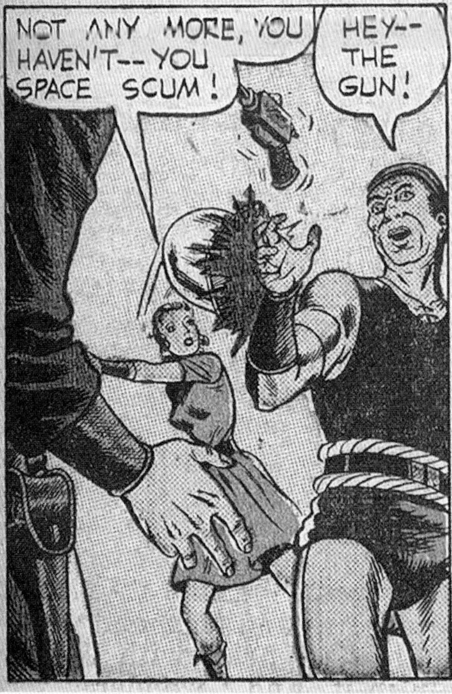
NOT ANY MORE, YOU HAVEN'T-- YOU SPACE SCUM!
HEY-- THE GUN!

OUT OF THIS WORLD

JET PLANES AND ROCKETS HAD MADE TRAVEL A MATTER OF MINUTES WHERE IT HAD PREVIOUSLY BEEN HOURS...THE WORLD BECAME SMALLER AND SMALLER...SO MAN EXPANDED HIS PIONEERING INTO THE TREMENDOUS FIELD OF SPACE ...BUT EVEN HERE HE FOUND IT WAS...

A SMALL WORLD

A MAN REACHED THE MOON IN 1962--RADIO SIGNALS CONTINUED FOR FOUR DAYS BEFORE HE APPARENTLY CEASED TO LIVE...

BY 1970, MAN TRAVELED TO THE MOON AND RETURNED TO EARTH--OTHER MEN EXPLORED SATURN AND JUPITER IN THE FOLLOWING DECADE...

BACK IN 1957, SPUTNICK KICKED OFF A CRASH PROGRAM IN EARTH'S ADVANCE INTO SPACE...

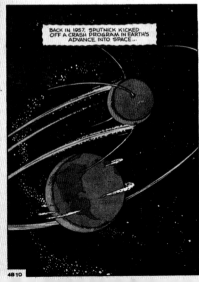

IN THE LATTER DAYS OF THE TWENTIETH CENTURY, THE SPACE-MAN LEARNED TO FACE NEW DANGERS...THE HORROR OF ABSOLUTE COLD...AND SEARING MOLTEN HEAT--AND HE FLED FOR HIS LIFE FROM UNNAMED HORRORS...AS COMMANDER GALT WAS NOW DOING!

I TOLD THEM I SAW MOVEMENT DOWN THERE BEFORE WE LANDED--THEY INSISTED THAT WE INVESTIGATE ANYHOW!

4810

GREAT MAN

PROFESSOR MADDEN of the Biology Department of City University faced his class with a slight smile. "We've spent the hour discussing the infallibility of scientific laws," he said, "and there's no better way of indicating my attitude on this question than by citing the recent experience of Dr. Amos Jason, the biotics expert who recently discovered the cure for swamp fever. He developed his serum on the scene, so to speak—carrying on his successful research in a small town near the Okeechobee Swamp which had periodically suffered from epidemics of swamp fever. He set up a laboratory which was staffed mainly by local folks, since few outsiders dared enter such a disease-ridden region.

"Our discussion here will be restricted to two widely differing members of Dr. Jason's staff. The first was Edward Rutley, son of the town pharmacist. Always a conscientious student as well as a member of one of the best families, Edward was a graduate of the State University, where he'd been an outstanding biology major. Dr. Jason counted himself lucky to have him as a lab assistant—a job to which he made notable contributions. The second staff member was a lowly one—Tom Simpson, the lab's janitor. Tom had sprung from poverty and was completely illiterate. All his life he had been in and out of trouble. People knew him as a lazy ne'er-do-well, and predicted he'd come to a bad end. Dr. Jason had occasion to rebuke him when he overheard him insolently refusing to clean up Ed Rutley's lab.

"Doc Jason was more than a bit short-tempered at the time, because his research had hit a snag. He was in no mood to stand for any of Simpson's crude nonsense, and he told him so. In his temper, he said a little too *much*. He told the janitor that he'd never rise above his station because he wouldn't try—because he was satisfied with the dirt and shiftless sloth from which he'd sprung. In contrast, he pointed out how Rutley had studied and striven, as had his family. And, ever the scientist, he used the situation to indicate how great a force was *environment*. In Simpson's case, a bad environment had produced an unfavorable specimen—whereas Rutley's background had served to create an excellent citizen. Dr. Jason knew he was going a bit overboard in this sweeping generalization, but he had a point to make. 'Rutley's a product of a fine environment,' he said, 'and he'll make a *great man!* But *you*, Simpson—you'll never rise above what produced you—nobody will ever remember you for anything good! And to show you that it's *environment* that counts, I checked into the history of all our workers. Your ancestors were members of the British peerage—brave soldiers, heroes—while Rutley came from farming folk! So you see, heredity doesn't mean very much!'

"'My ancestors—*royalty*? Soldiers an'—an' *heroes*?' Simpson's tones were dazed, unbelieving. There was a difference in him as he went about his work in the succeeding weeks, but Dr. Jason had no time to notice it. With Ed Rutley's help, he had made great progress in his serum—it had almost reached the stage where it could be administered. But just at this time, a deadly epidemic of swamp fever struck the region. Death followed death in alarming proportions. There was only one thing that might save the remnants of the populace, and that was the new serum. Dr. Jason had no doubt that it would prove effective—but there was the great fear that it might prove too strong for human use. There was only one way to find out—would a volunteer come forward? But the dangers were too great, and nobody dared take the fearful chance. Helplessly, Dr. Jason looked towards Rutley—who flinched and turned away. Then it was that Tom Simpson stepped forward. *"You?"* asked Jason incredulously. "Don't you know the *risk*? Why are you doing this?" But Simpson doggedly refused to answer. Bravely, he submitted to injection.

"I wish I could say that it turned out well as far as the poor janitor was concerned, but it didn't. As Dr. Jason had feared, the serum proved too strong for human use. And as he kept a death vigil at Simpson's bedside, he heard the dying man mutter, 'Royalty . . . *heroes* . . . ' Only that—before he closed his eyes forever."

Professor Madden concluded his story, and one of his students broke the silence. "Is your point that heredity is, after all, greater than *environment?*" he asked. The Professor shook his head. "You'll find adherents on both sides of *that* question," he said. "So let's say that whatever the answer, Simpson *was* a hero, a great man—and science is great because sometimes, it admits the fallibility of its own laws!"

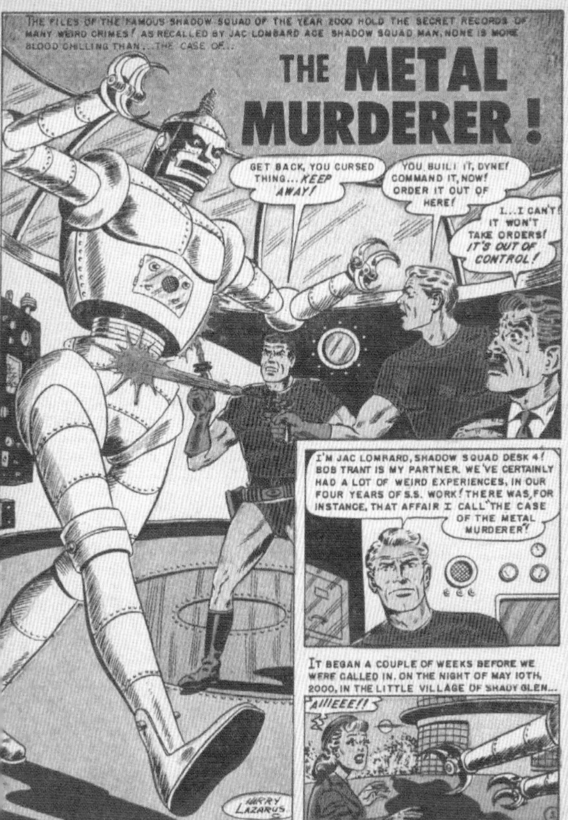
THE FILES OF THE FAMOUS SHADOW SQUAD OF THE YEAR 2000 HOLD THE SECRET RECORDS OF MANY WEIRD CRIMES! AS RECALLED BY JAC LOMBARD ACE SHADOW SQUAD MAN, NONE IS MORE BLOOD CHILLING THAN... THE CASE OF...
THE METAL MURDERER!
GET BACK, YOU CURSED THING... KEEP AWAY!
YOU BUILT IT, DYNE! COMMAND IT, NOW! ORDER IT OUT OF HERE!
I... I CAN'T! IT WON'T TAKE ORDERS! IT'S OUT OF CONTROL!
HARRY LAZARUS
I'M JAC LOMRARD, SHADOW SQUAD DESK 4! BOB TRANT IS MY PARTNER. WE'VE CERTAINLY HAD A LOT OF WEIRD EXPERIENCES, IN OUR FOUR YEARS OF S.S. WORK! THERE WAS, FOR INSTANCE, THAT AFFAIR I CALL "THE CASE OF THE METAL MURDERER"!
IT BEGAN A COUPLE OF WEEKS BEFORE WE WERE CALLED IN. ON THE NIGHT OF MAY 10TH, 2000, IN THE LITTLE VILLAGE OF SHADY GLEN...
AIIIEEE!!

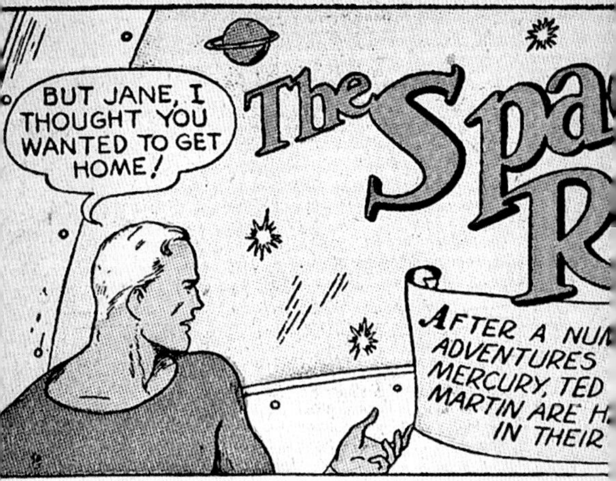
BUT JANE, I THOUGHT YOU WANTED TO GET HOME!
The
AFTER A
ADVENTURES
MERCURY, TED
MARTIN ARE
IN THEIR

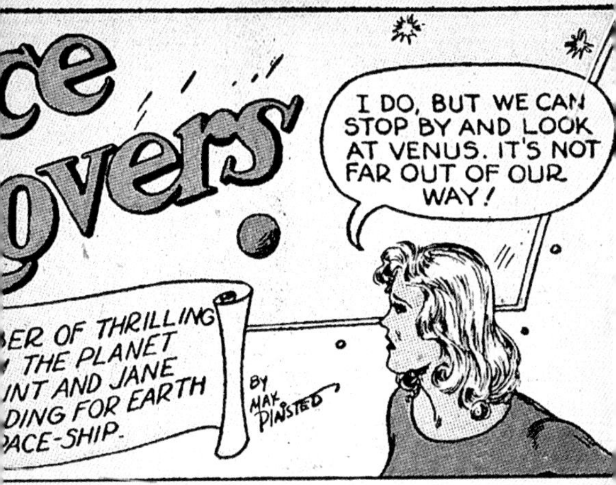
ce
overs
ER OF THRILLING
THE PLANET
INT AND JANE
DING FOR EARTH
ACE-SHIP.
BY MAX PLAISTED
I DO, BUT WE CAN STOP BY AND LOOK AT VENUS. IT'S NOT FAR OUT OF OUR WAY!

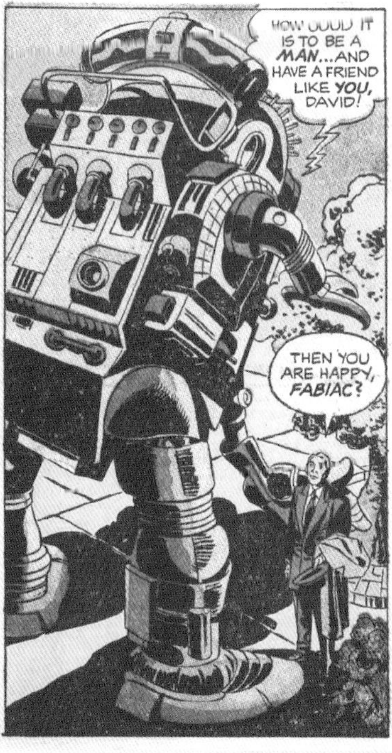
HOW GOOD IT IS TO BE A *MAN*...AND HAVE A FRIEND LIKE *YOU*, DAVID!
THEN YOU ARE HAPPY, *FABIAC*?

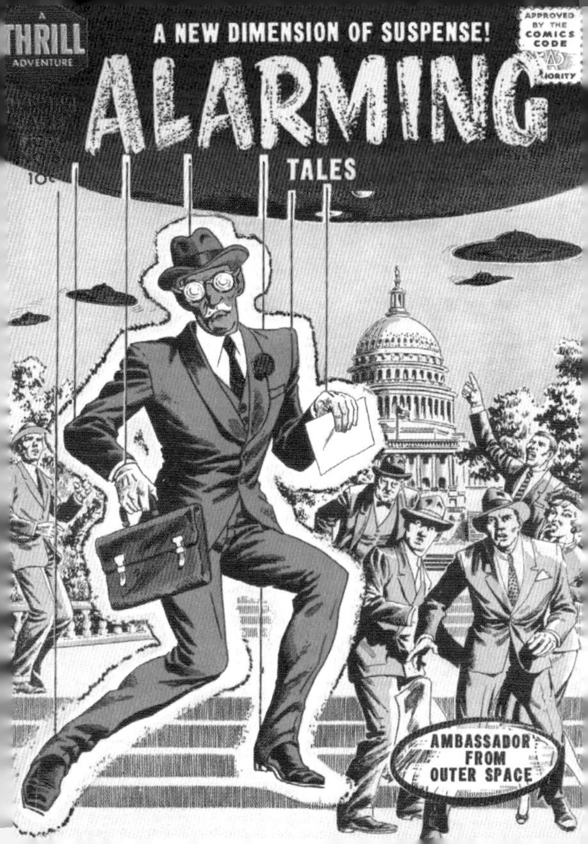
A THRILL ADVENTURE
A NEW DIMENSION OF SUSPENSE!
APPROVED BY THE COMICS CODE
ALARMING
TALES
10¢
AMBASSADOR FROM OUTER SPACE

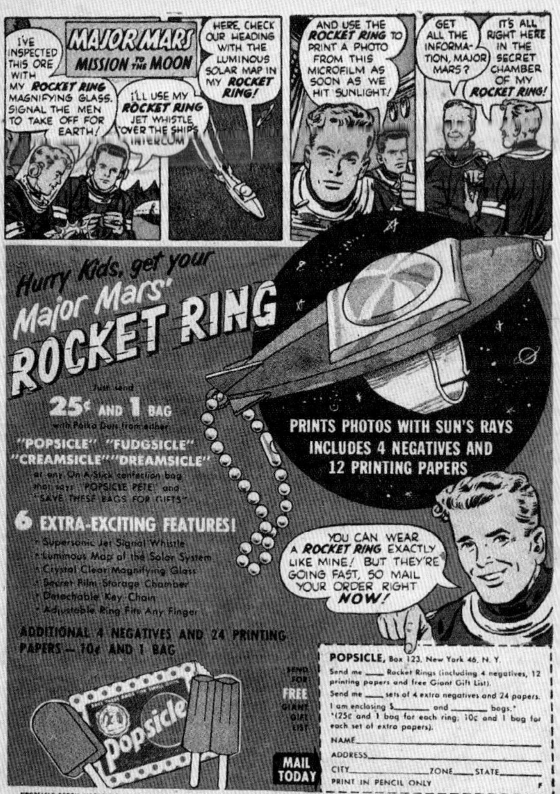
MAJOR MARS
MISSION TO THE MOON
I'VE INSPECTED THIS ORE WITH MY ROCKET RING MAGNIFYING GLASS. SIGNAL THE MEN TO TAKE OFF FOR EARTH!
I'LL USE MY ROCKET RING JET WHISTLE OVER THE SHIPS INTERCOM
HERE, CHECK OUR HEADING WITH THE LUMINOUS SOLAR MAP IN MY ROCKET RING!
AND USE THE ROCKET RING TO PRINT A PHOTO FROM THIS MICROFILM AS SOON AS WE HIT SUNLIGHT!
GET ALL THE INFORMATION, MAJOR MARS?
IT'S ALL RIGHT HERE IN THE SECRET CHAMBER OF MY ROCKET RING!
Hurry Kids, get your
Major Mars'
ROCKET RING
Just send
25¢ AND 1 BAG
with Polka Dots from either
"POPSICLE" "FUDGSICLE"
"CREAMSICLE" "DREAMSICLE"
or any On-A-Stick confection bag that says "POPSICLE PETE" and "SAVE THESE BAGS FOR GIFTS"
6 EXTRA-EXCITING FEATURES!
• Supersonic Jet Signal Whistle
• Luminous Map of the Solar System
• Crystal Clear Magnifying Glass
• Secret Film Storage Chamber
• Detachable Key Chain
• Adjustable Ring Fits Any Finger
ADDITIONAL 4 NEGATIVES AND 24 PRINTING PAPERS — 10¢ AND 1 BAG
PRINTS PHOTOS WITH SUN'S RAYS
INCLUDES 4 NEGATIVES AND
12 PRINTING PAPERS
YOU CAN WEAR A ROCKET RING EXACTLY LIKE MINE! BUT THEY'RE GOING FAST, SO MAIL YOUR ORDER RIGHT NOW!
Popsicle
SEND FOR FREE GIANT GIFT LIST
MAIL TODAY
POPSICLE, Box 123, New York 46, N. Y.
Send me ____ Rocket Rings (including 4 negatives, 12 printing papers and free Giant Gift List).
Send me ____ sets of 4 extra negatives and 24 papers.
I am enclosing $________ and ________ bags.*
*(25¢ and 1 bag for each ring; 10¢ and 1 bag for each set of extra papers).
NAME
ADDRESS
CITY ZONE STATE
PRINT IN PENCIL ONLY
F

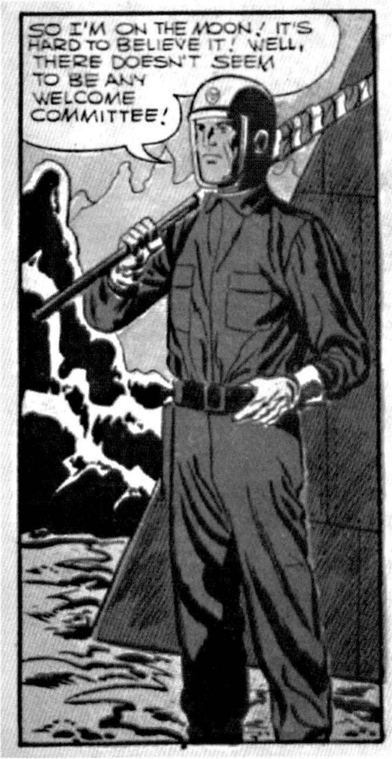
SO I'M ON THE MOON! IT'S HARD TO BELIEVE IT! WELL, THERE DOESN'T SEEM TO BE ANY WELCOME COMMITTEE!

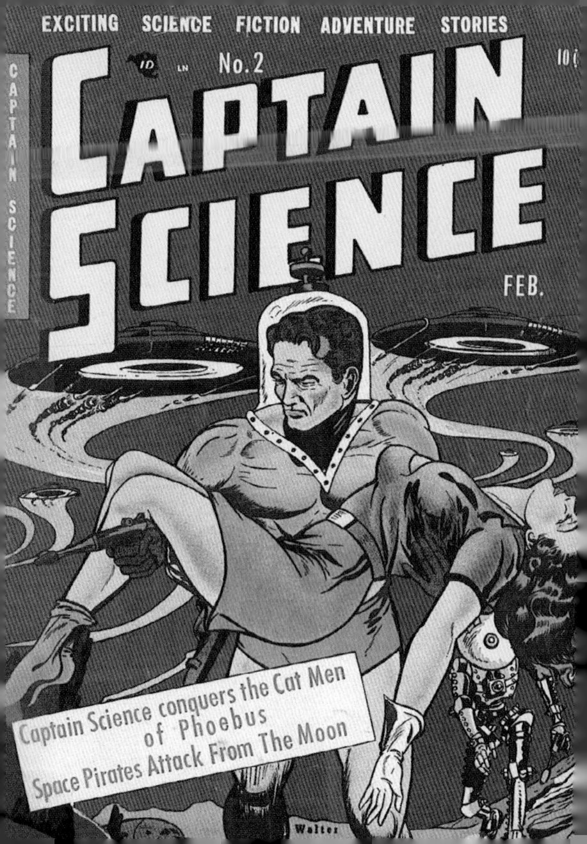

EXCITING SCIENCE FICTION ADVENTURE STORIES
No. 2
10¢
CAPTAIN SCIENCE
FEB.
CAPTAIN SCIENCE
Captain Science conquers the Cat Men of Phoebus
Space Pirates Attack From The Moon

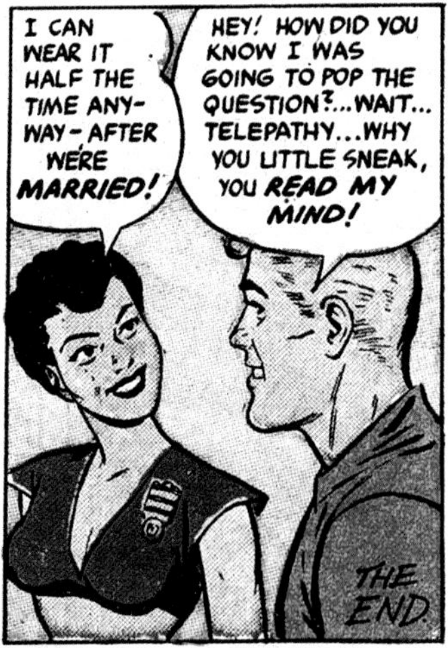
I CAN WEAR IT HALF THE TIME ANY-WAY - AFTER WE'RE MARRIED!
HEY! HOW DID YOU KNOW I WAS GOING TO POP THE QUESTION?...WAIT... TELEPATHY...WHY YOU LITTLE SNEAK, YOU READ MY MIND!
THE END

ELUDING THE VENUSIAN POLICE THE GANG TAKES CRAIG TO THEIR HIDEOUT, WHERE HE IS INTRODUCED TO THE "BOSS"...
THIS SPACE JOCKEY HATES THE PATROL, FIGHTS LIKE A MARTIAN LION AND IS PLENTY TOUGH. WE CAN USE HIM.
YEAH? YOU LIKE TO JOIN UP WITH US, FELLOW?
MAYBE. WHAT HAVE YOU GOT TO OFFER?

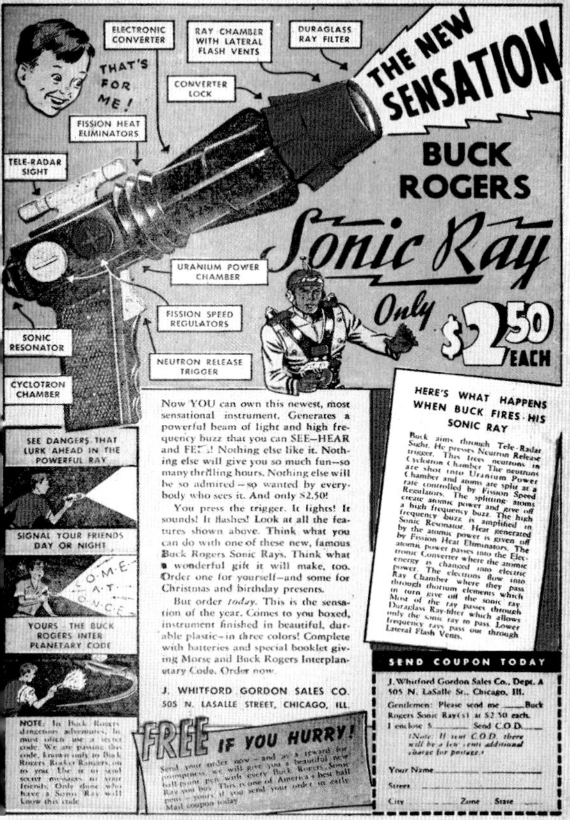
ELECTRONIC CONVERTER
RAY CHAMBER WITH LATERAL FLASH VENTS
DURAGLASS RAY FILTER
THAT'S FOR ME!
CONVERTER LOCK
FISSION HEAT ELIMINATORS
TELE-RADAR SIGHT
THE NEW SENSATION
BUCK ROGERS
Sonic Ray
URANIUM POWER CHAMBER
FISSION SPEED REGULATORS
Only $2.50 EACH
SONIC RESONATOR
NEUTRON RELEASE TRIGGER
CYCLOTRON CHAMBER
Now YOU can own this newest, most sensational instrument. Generates a powerful beam of light and high frequency buzz that you can SEE—HEAR and FE ! Nothing else like it. Nothing else will give you so much fun—so many thrilling hours. Nothing else will be so admired—so wanted by everybody who sees it. And only $2.50!
You press the trigger. It lights! It sounds! It flashes! Look at all the features shown above. Think what you can do with one of these new, famous Buck Rogers Sonic Rays. Think what a wonderful gift it will make, too. Order one for yourself—and some for Christmas and birthday presents.
But order *today*. This is the sensation of the year. Comes to you boxed, instrument finished in beautiful, durable plastic—in three colors! Complete with batteries and special booklet giving Morse and Buck Rogers Interplanetary Code. Order now.
J. WHITFORD GORDON SALES CO.
505 N. LASALLE STREET, CHICAGO, ILL.
HERE'S WHAT HAPPENS WHEN BUCK FIRES HIS SONIC RAY
Buck aims through Tele-Radar Sight. He presses Neutron Release trigger. This frees neutrons in Cyclotron Chamber. The neutrons are shot into Uranium Power Chamber and atoms are split at a rate controlled by Fission Speed Regulators. The splitting atoms create atomic power and give off a high frequency buzz. The high frequency buzz is amplified in Sonic Resonator. Heat generated by the atomic power is given off by Fission Heat Eliminators. The atomic power passes into the Electronic Converter where the atomic energy is changed into electric power. The electrons flow into Ray Chamber where they pass through thorium elements which in turn give off the sonic ray. Most of the ray passes through Duraglass Ray-filter which allows only the sonic ray to pass. Lower frequency rays pass out through Lateral Flash Vents.
SEE DANGERS THAT LURK AHEAD IN THE POWERFUL RAY
SIGNAL YOUR FRIENDS DAY OR NIGHT
C-O-M-E A-T O-N-C-E
YOURS — THE BUCK ROGERS INTER PLANETARY CODE
NOTE: In Buck Rogers dangerous adventures, he must often use a secret code. We are passing this code, known only to Buck Rogers Rocket Rangers, on to you. Use it to send secret messages to your friends. Only those who have a Sonic Ray will know this code.
FREE IF YOU HURRY!
Send your order now—and as a reward for promptness, we will give you a beautiful new ball-point pen with every Buck Rogers Sonic Ray you buy. This is one of America's best ball pens—yours if you send your order in early. Mail coupon today.
SEND COUPON TODAY
J. Whitford Gordon Sales Co., Dept. A
505 N. LaSalle St., Chicago, Ill.
Gentlemen: Please send me ____ Buck Rogers Sonic Ray(s) at $2.50 each.
I enclose $_____ Send C.O.D.____
(Note: If sent C.O.D. there will be a few cents additional charge for postage.)
Your Name __________
Street __________
City _____ Zone ___ State ___

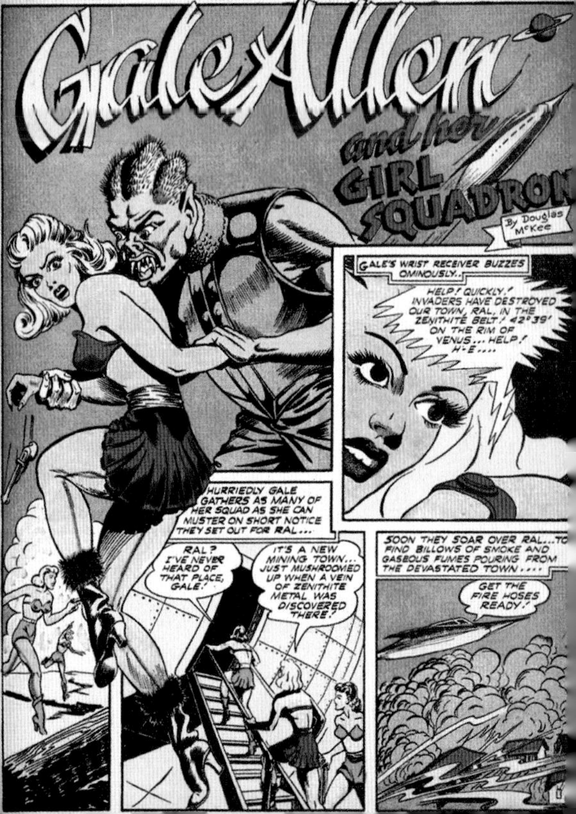
Gale Allen and her GIRL SQUADRON
By Douglas McKee
GALE'S WRIST RECEIVER BUZZES OMINOUSLY..
HELP! QUICKLY! INVADERS HAVE DESTROYED OUR TOWN, RAL, IN THE ZENITHITE BELT! 42°39' ON THE RIM OF VENUS... HELP! H-E....
HURRIEDLY GALE GATHERS AS MANY OF HER SQUAD AS SHE CAN MUSTER ON SHORT NOTICE THEY SET OUT FOR RAL...
RAL? I'VE NEVER HEARD OF THAT PLACE, GALE!
IT'S A NEW MINING TOWN... JUST MUSHROOMED UP WHEN A VEIN OF ZENITHITE METAL WAS DISCOVERED THERE!
SOON THEY SOAR OVER RAL...TO FIND BILLOWS OF SMOKE AND GASEOUS FUMES POURING FROM THE DEVASTATED TOWN....
GET THE FIRE HOSES READY!

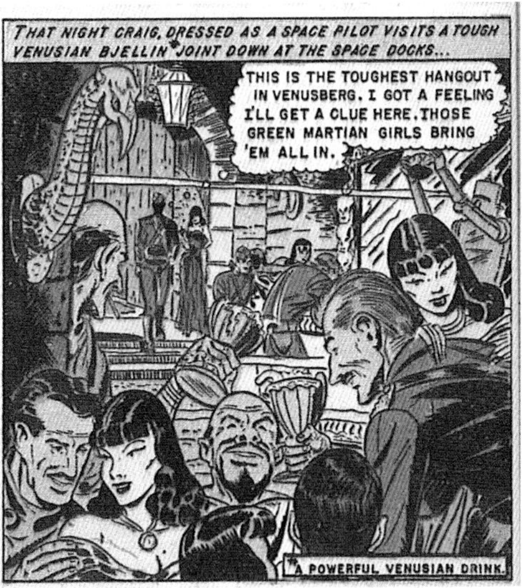
THAT NIGHT CRAIG, DRESSED AS A SPACE PILOT VISITS A TOUGH VENUSIAN BJELLIN* JOINT DOWN AT THE SPACE DOCKS...
THIS IS THE TOUGHEST HANGOUT IN VENUSBERG. I GOT A FEELING I'LL GET A CLUE HERE. THOSE GREEN MARTIAN GIRLS BRING 'EM ALL IN.
*A POWERFUL VENUSIAN DRINK.

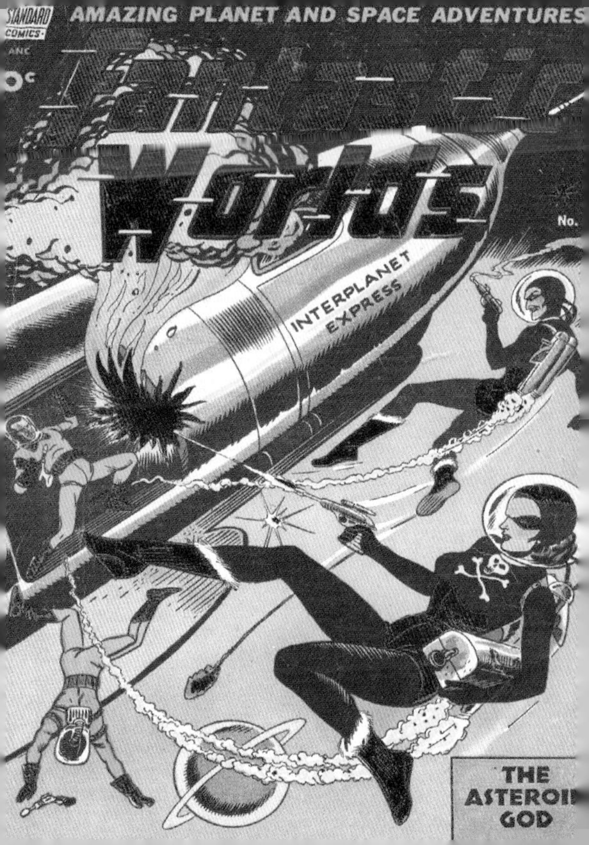
STANDARD COMICS
AMAZING PLANET AND SPACE ADVENTURES
Worlds
No.
INTERPLANET EXPRESS
THE ASTEROI GOD

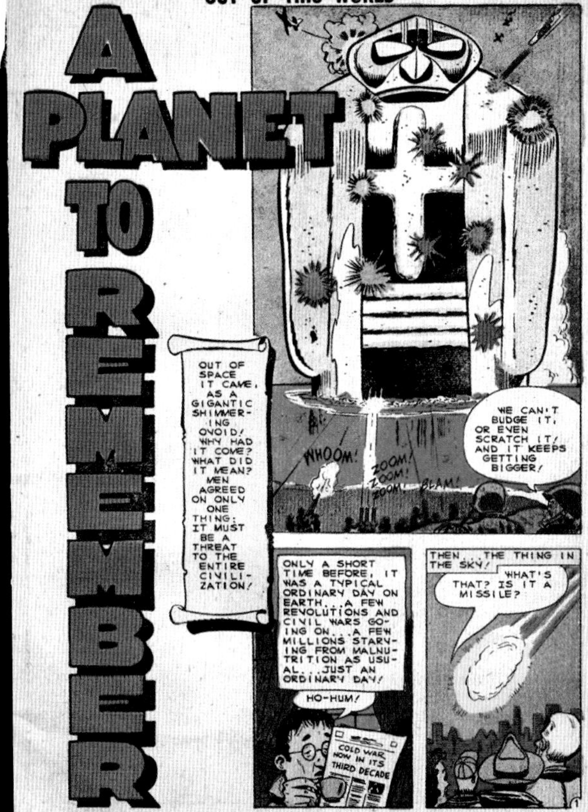
A PLANET TO REMEMBER
OUT OF SPACE IT CAME, AS A GIGANTIC SHIMMERING OVOID! WHY HAD IT COME? WHAT DID IT MEAN? MEN AGREED ON ONLY ONE THING: IT MUST BE A THREAT TO THE ENTIRE CIVILIZATION!
WHOOM!
ZOOM! ZOOM! ZOOM!
BLAM!
WE CAN'T BUDGE IT, OR EVEN SCRATCH IT! AND IT KEEPS GETTING BIGGER!
ONLY A SHORT TIME BEFORE, IT WAS A TYPICAL ORDINARY DAY ON EARTH... A FEW REVOLUTIONS AND CIVIL WARS GOING ON... A FEW MILLIONS STARVING FROM MALNUTRITION AS USUAL... JUST AN ORDINARY DAY!
HO-HUM!
COLD WAR NOW IN ITS THIRD DECADE
THEN... THE THING IN THE SKY!
WHAT'S THAT? IS IT A MISSILE?
1

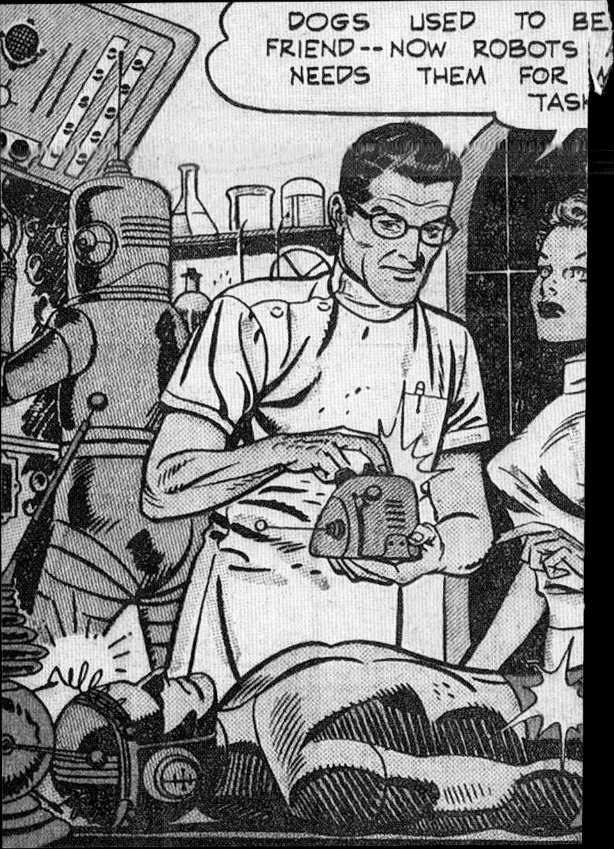
DOGS USED TO BE
FRIEND--NOW ROBOTS
NEEDS THEM FOR
TASK

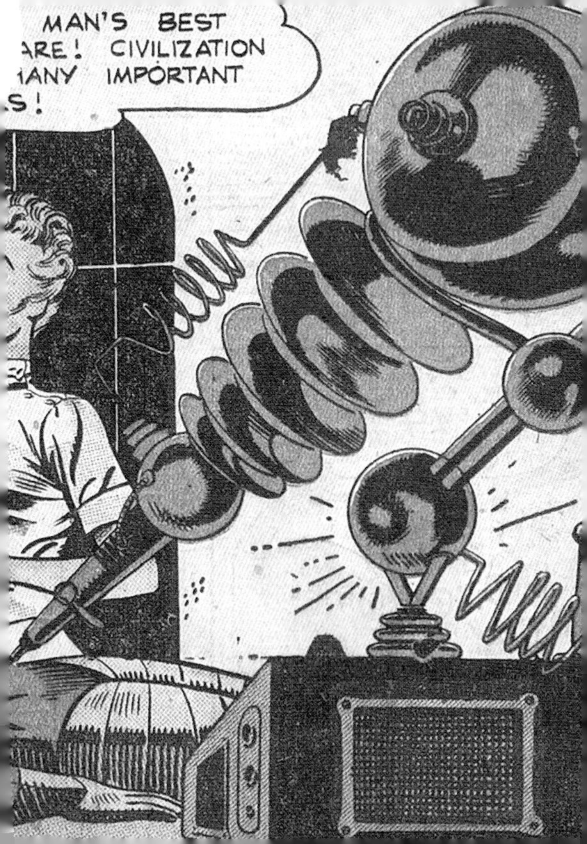
MAN'S BEST
ARE! CIVILIZATION
MANY IMPORTANT
S!

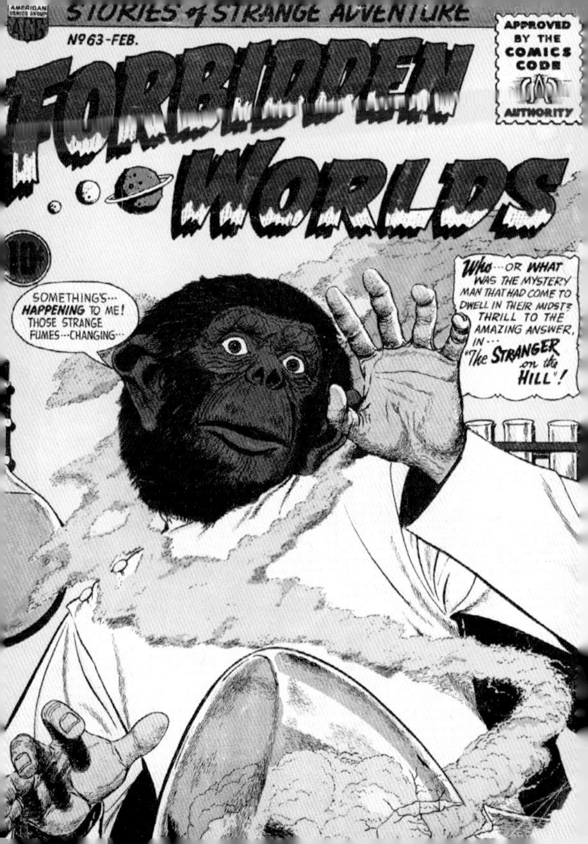
AMERICAN COMICS GROUP
ACG
STORIES of STRANGE ADVENTURE
Nº63-FEB.
FORBIDDEN WORLDS
APPROVED BY THE COMICS CODE AUTHORITY
10¢
SOMETHING'S--- HAPPENING TO ME! THOSE STRANGE FUMES---CHANGING---
Who---OR WHAT WAS THE MYSTERY MAN THAT HAD COME TO DWELL IN THEIR MIDST? THRILL TO THE AMAZING ANSWER, IN--- "The STRANGER on the HILL"!

NEW! 1953 "Space Commander"

VIBRO-MATIC WALKIE-TALKIES

2 PHONES ONLY $1

2 WAY
SENDS! RECEIVES!
VOICE - SONGS - MUSIC

Thrills & Fun Galore!

If by some magical means you could talk with your neighbor and friends—without electric wires, without batteries or electgic current, wouldn't you pay $100 or more? Well you can do just that and the entire cost to you is only ONE DOLLAR for TWO "Space Commander" Walkie-Talkies. Not just a toy—but an amazing communication system. NOW you can talk back and forth from house to garden, between rooms, between your house and your friends'. How thrilling to "speak thru space"!

Works like Magic . . . Guaranteed!

This latest, newest 1953 model is a well made product of the world's largest manufacturer of Walkie-Talkies. Uses highly sensitive Vibromatic design. Each phone is self-contained and sends as well as receives messages, songs, music, etc. which travel over the conductor line for hundreds of feet, clear and distinct. Requires no license. Will not interfere with radio reception. Works equally well indoors or out.

Endless Fun . . . Educational!

This new 2-WAY WalkieTalkie System provides endless fun for the entire family, for boys and girls and adults too! Inspirational. Helps overcome shyness, aids voice training. Real "Space Planet" design in handsome colors. Hard to break. They're rugged!

5 Day Trial — Money Back Guarantee.

Send only one dollar, cash, check or money order and your Walkie-Talkies will be shipped on 5 day home trial—instantly! Easy to use directions—even a 5-year-old child can do it! Enjoy them with your family and friends for 5 whole days free of any obligation to keep them . . . entirely at our risk! If you're not thrilled and satisfied in every way your dollar comes right back! Supply limited! Rush order now! Don't lose this big bargain! Mail coupon TODAY!

CONSUMERS MART, Dept. 153-#-28
131 West 33rd Street, New York 1, N. Y.

SPECIAL!

$1 : 2 PHONES COMPLETE

Rush this MONEY-SAVING COUPON

CONSUMERS MART, Dept. 153-#-28
131 West 33rd Street, New York 1, N. Y.

RUSH a complete set of SPACE COMMANDER WALKIE-TALKIES on 5 DAY TRIAL, post-paid. I enclose only $1.00 for the complete set of 2 phones and directions. If I am not thrilled and satisfied in every way, you are to send back my dollar with no questions asked.

NAME ______________________

ADDRESS ______________________

TOWN ______________ STATE ______________

☐ CHECK here if you wish order sent C.O.D. You pay $1.00 AND 35 cents postage on delivery.

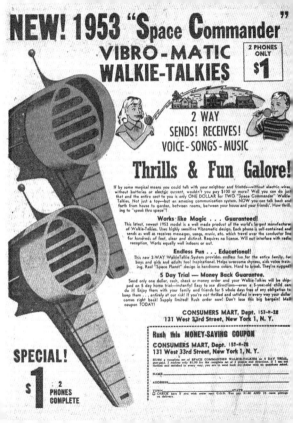

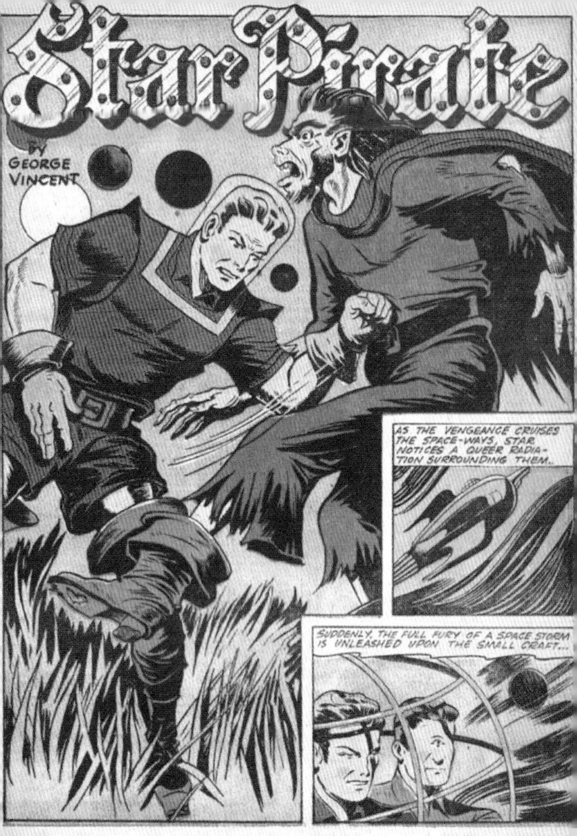
Star Pirate
BY GEORGE VINCENT
AS THE VENGEANCE CRUISES THE SPACE-WAYS, STAR NOTICES A QUEER RADIATION SURROUNDING THEM..
SUDDENLY, THE FULL FURY OF A SPACE STORM IS UNLEASHED UPON THE SMALL CRAFT...

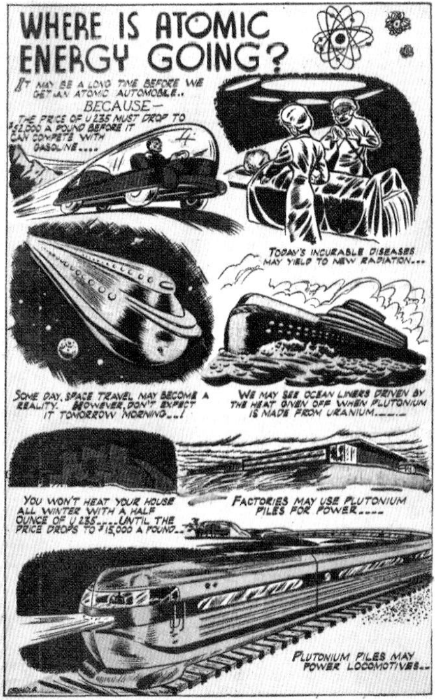
WHERE IS ATOMIC ENERGY GOING?
IT MAY BE A LONG TIME BEFORE WE GET AN ATOMIC AUTOMOBILE..
BECAUSE—
THE PRICE OF U 235 MUST DROP TO $2,000 A POUND BEFORE IT CAN COMPETE WITH GASOLINE....
TODAY'S INCURABLE DISEASES MAY YIELD TO NEW RADIATION...
SOME DAY, SPACE TRAVEL MAY BECOME A REALITY. HOWEVER, DON'T EXPECT IT TOMORROW MORNING...!
WE MAY SEE OCEAN LINERS DRIVEN BY THE HEAT GIVEN OFF WHEN PLUTONIUM IS MADE FROM URANIUM.....
YOU WON'T HEAT YOUR HOUSE ALL WINTER WITH A HALF OUNCE OF U 235.....UNTIL THE PRICE DROPS TO $15,000 A POUND...
FACTORIES MAY USE PLUTONIUM PILES FOR POWER....
PLUTONIUM PILES MAY POWER LOCOMOTIVES...

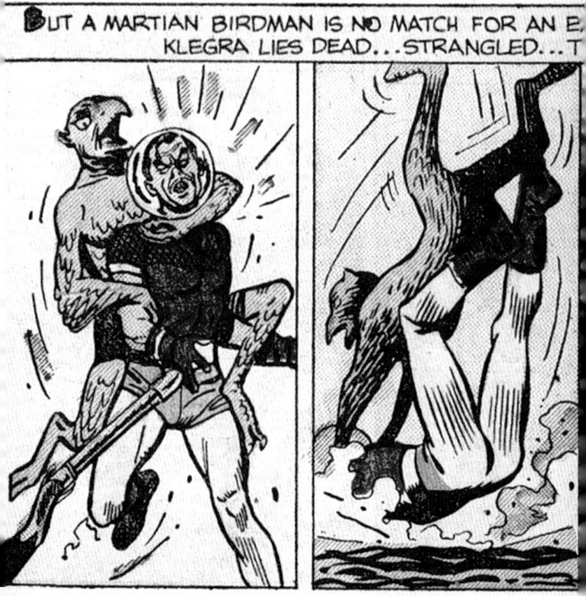
BUT A MARTIAN BIRDMAN IS NO MATCH FOR AN E
KLEGRA LIES DEAD...STRANGLED...T

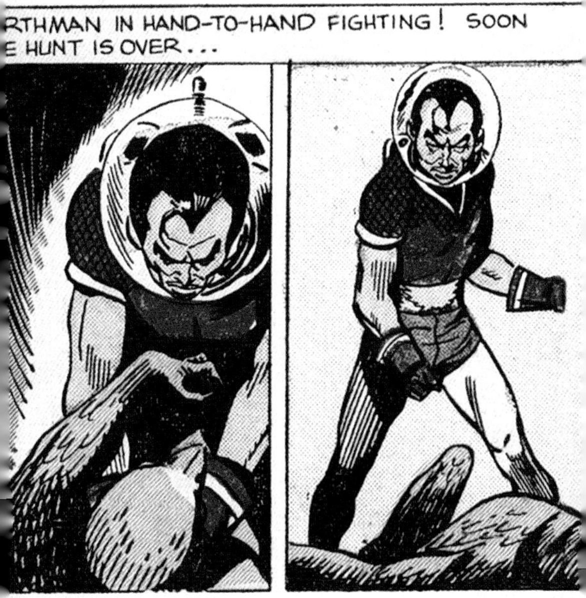
RTHMAN IN HAND-TO-HAND FIGHTING! SOON
E HUNT IS OVER...

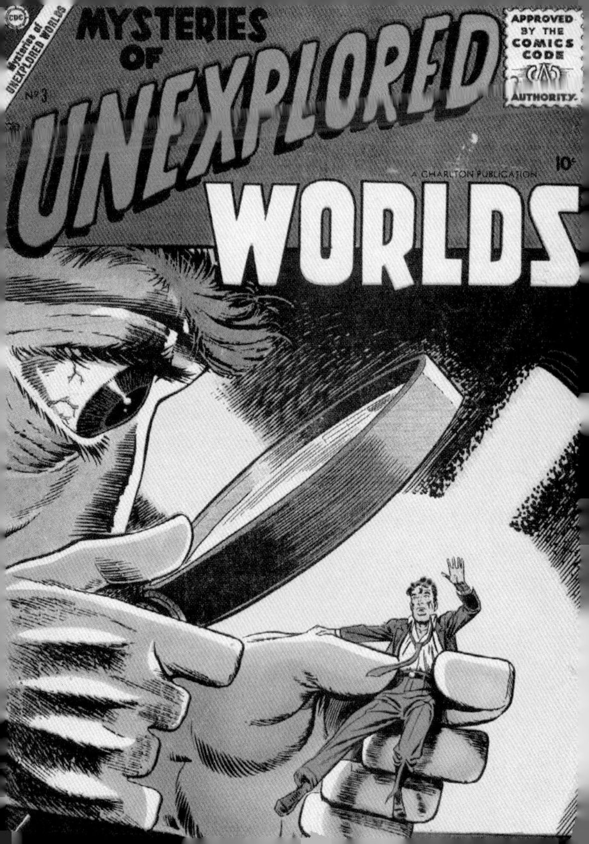
Mysteries of UNEXPLORED WORLDS
MYSTERIES OF UNEXPLORED WORLDS
Nº 3
APPROVED BY THE COMICS CODE AUTHORITY
10¢
A CHARLTON PUBLICATION

WEIRD VALLEY

It's always a bad idea to divide authority, and this proved particularly true with regard to the Civic Museum's polar expedition. It was led by two men, Brian Connors and Ned Gordon. Ned was mild and easygoing, but Brian Connors was an impatient, domineering type. It was due to his insistence that the expedition wandered from its prescribed route and became hopelessly lost in the frigid Artic.

Their supplies gave out as they wandered aimlessly through the blizzard-wracked wasteland and they were starving and almost out of their heads when they were rescued by a small group of nomadic Eskimos.

Old Belora was the headman. He gave them food and shelter and saw that they were nursed back to health. And during the period of their convalescence, he told them many stories of the strange phenomena of the northland—stories to which Ned Gordon listened with bated breath. But Brian Connors scorned them, privately labeling them as tall stories and nothing more.

They told the old man that as soon as they were strong again and re-equipped with food, they would strike out again, heading due north into territory never before explored. They wondered about the look of fear that spread across the old man's face, and why he was so vehement in warning them not to venture into that territory. It would mean their certain deaths, he told them, but he wouldn't say why.

But Connors thought he *knew* why. All the Eskimos, strangely, wore armbands of a raw, beaten yellow material which could only be pure gold. Obviously, he said, they had gotten the precious metal in the very area from which Belora was warning them. He told the old man that no matter what he said, they intended to take the northward course.

It was at this point that the old Eskimo leader broke down and told them the story. He had been sworn to secrecy, he said, and was only revealing the facts to save them from extinction.

For due north lay the forbidden valley, a geologic flaw in the polar cap. It was a large valley, surrounded by tall cliffs—and below its floor was a huge volcanic stratum which heated it and made of it a green oasis amid the snowy wastes. In consequence, it had maintained through the countless centuries the very same vegetation and animal life that had pertained a million years ago. And within the valley, there dwelled a race of giant white men that had domesticated the animals, using some to guard the valley and its approaches. For they wished no interlopers from the outside world to invade their rich and beautiful valley.

As for Belora and his people, they were in favor with the white giants, for on several occasions, the Eskimos had rescued giants who had ventured outside the valley and been overcome by the cold. It was for this that they had been given the priceless gold ornaments—obviously, gold in profusion existed within the forbidden land.

It was a strange story, but there might be some truth in it, so none of the expedition headed that way—none but Connors, who was obviously spellbound by the gold. For when the members of the expedition awoke in the morning, he was gone, and there wasn't any doubt of his destination. "We've got to go after him." said Ned Gordon. "There's no telling what trouble he may get into!"

Heading due north, they pushed on at all speed. "He doesn't believe Belora's story." said Gordon. "All he believes is that there's gold there, and he's after it. Let's speed it up—I wouldn't want anything to happen to him!"

They pressed on and on—and finally, a circle of mountains came into view, which obviously ringed the storied valley. Following Connors' trail, they began the steep upward climb. From a distance, far above, there came a thrashing sound, a despairing cry.

"Faster!" cried Gordon. "That—that was Connors' voice!" Far ahead, they saw it now—that dark spot on the snow. When they reached it, it was Connors. He was dead, mauled by some creature of gigantic strength. "That story was *true*," breathed one of the men. "One of the giants must have gotten him!" But Gordon shook his head. "Look!" he said, pointing upward. "It was truer than you think!"

The members of the expedition looked in the direction in which he was pointing. Far above, something was surmounting the rocky barrier, about to plod downward into the valley itself. *It was a huge dinosaur!*

DO YOU FEEL AS WARM AS I DO?
WE'RE PROBABLY NEARING A MINOR SUN! WE MUST GET INTO OUR ASBESTOS SPACE SUITS!

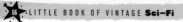

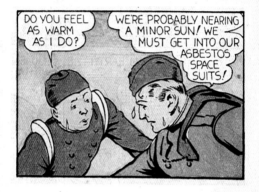

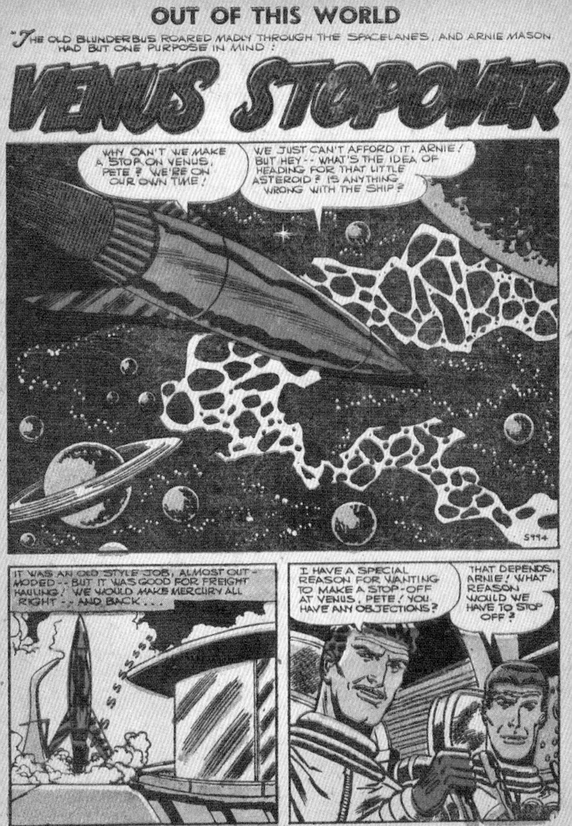
OUT OF THIS WORLD
"THE OLD BLUNDERBUS ROARED MADLY THROUGH THE SPACELANES, AND ARNIE MASON HAD BUT ONE PURPOSE IN MIND :
VENUS STOPOVER
WHY CAN'T WE MAKE A STOP ON VENUS, PETE ? WE'RE ON OUR OWN TIME !
WE JUST CAN'T AFFORD IT, ARNIE ! BUT HEY -- WHAT'S THE IDEA OF HEADING FOR THAT LITTLE ASTEROID ? IS ANYTHING WRONG WITH THE SHIP ?
IT WAS AN OLD STYLE JOB, ALMOST OUT-MODED -- BUT IT WAS GOOD FOR FREIGHT HAULING ! WE WOULD MAKE MERCURY ALL RIGHT -- AND BACK ...
SSSSSSSSS
I HAVE A SPECIAL REASON FOR WANTING TO MAKE A STOP-OFF AT VENUS, PETE ! YOU HAVE ANY OBJECTIONS ?
THAT DEPENDS, ARNIE ! WHAT REASON WOULD WE HAVE TO STOP OFF ?

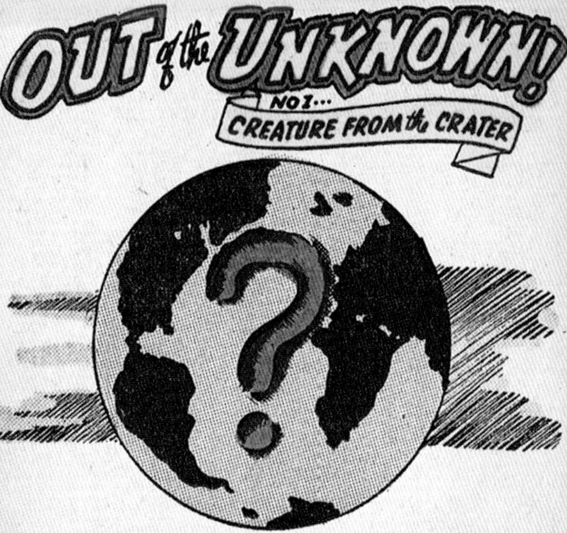
OUT of the UNKNOWN!
NO 1...
CREATURE FROM the CRATER

THE OFFICE OF THE CURATOR OF THE GEOLOGIC MUSEUM...
IT'S SETTLED, THEN ...OUR EXPEDITION WILL SET OUT ON JULY 16TH!
I STILL SAY THE WHOLE PROJECT'S RIDICULOUS! THE VERY IDEA... INVESTIGATING STORIES OF STRANGE CREATURES SAID TO HAVE ONCE LIVED INSIDE THE KOLARI VOLCANO!

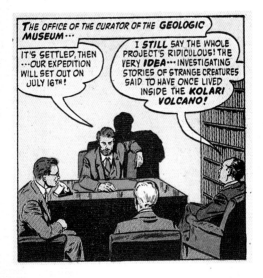

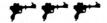

THE VOLCANO, EXTINCT FOR CENTURIES, LAY IN THE HEART OF THE SUMATRAN JUNGLE! THERE---AN AMAZING DISCOVERY!
THAT FOOTPRINT--- IT'S COMING OUT OF THE CRATER!
IT'S GIGANTIC---AND LOOKS ALMOST HUMAN! IT MUST HAVE BEEN MADE CENTURIES AGO, WHEN THE VOLCANO LAST ERUPTED--- BY SOME CREATURE ABLE TO WALK IN MOLTEN LAVA!

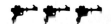

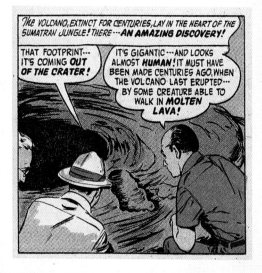

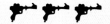

AT ONCE, THEY COMMENCED DIGGING NEARBY···

I DON'T BELIEVE THAT FOOTPRINT··· AND I THINK THAT EXCAVATING IS A WASTE OF TIME!

THOSE STONES WE FOUND AT THIS SPOT LOOK CARVED··· AS IF THEY'D ONCE BEEN USED AS *IMPLEMENTS* OF SOME SORT! IT WON'T HURT DIGGING DOWN JUST A *LITTLE!*

IT WAS THEN THAT THEY MADE THEIR FIND...
BONES... OF SOMEONE... OR SOMETHING...
LET'S BRING THEM BACK TO CAMP AND CHECK ON THEM!

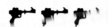

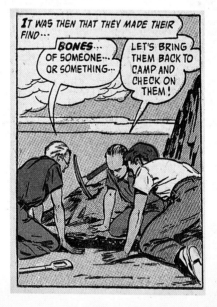

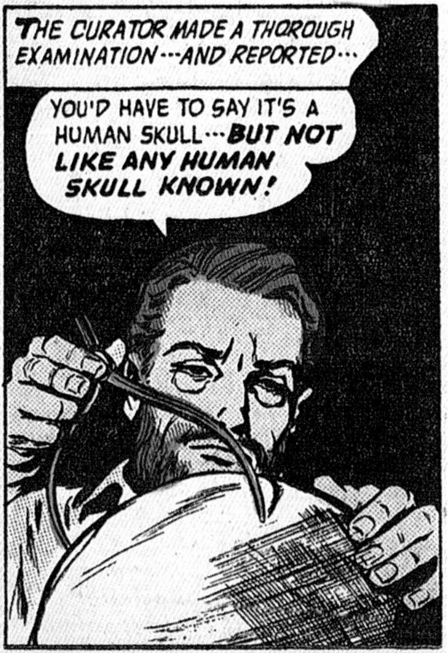
THE CURATOR MADE A THOROUGH EXAMINATION---AND REPORTED---
YOU'D HAVE TO SAY IT'S A HUMAN SKULL---BUT NOT LIKE ANY HUMAN SKULL KNOWN!

BUT ONE FINAL TEST REMAINED...

THE BONE HASN'T PETRIFIED, BUT IT'S COMPLETELY *IMPERVIOUS TO FIRE!* WHICH IS JUST ABOUT WHAT YOU MIGHT EXPECT FROM A CREATURE THAT *LIVED IN THE DEPTHS OF A FIERY VOLCANO!*

DID SUCH A CREATURE REALLY EXIST? WHAT DO YOU THINK, READER?

The END!

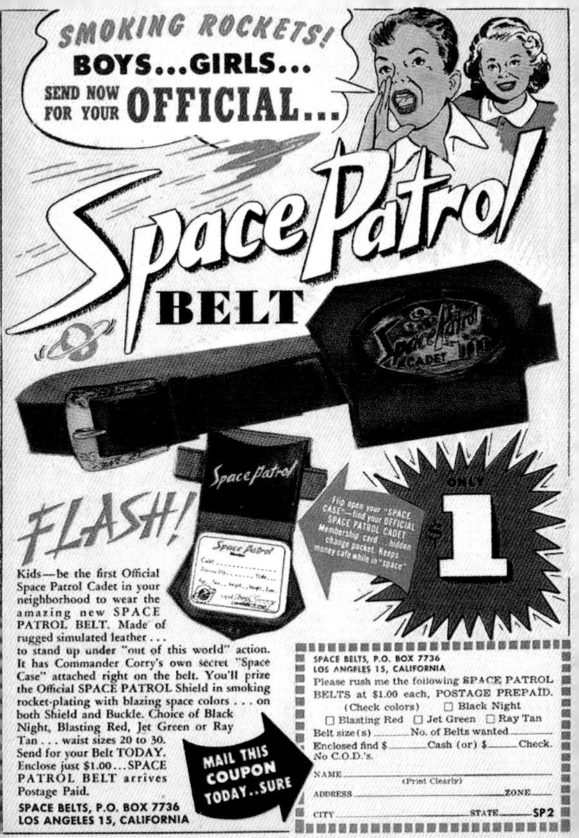
SMOKING ROCKETS!
BOYS...GIRLS...
SEND NOW FOR YOUR OFFICIAL...
Space Patrol
BELT
Space Patrol
FLASH!
Flip open your "SPACE CASE"—find your OFFICIAL SPACE PATROL CADET Membership card... hidden change pocket. Keeps money safe while in "space"
ONLY $1
Kids—be the first Official Space Patrol Cadet in your neighborhood to wear the amazing new SPACE PATROL BELT. Made of rugged simulated leather . . . to stand up under "out of this world" action. It has Commander Corry's own secret "Space Case" attached right on the belt. You'll prize the Official SPACE PATROL Shield in smoking rocket-plating with blazing space colors . . . on both Shield and Buckle. Choice of Black Night, Blasting Red, Jet Green or Ray Tan . . . waist sizes 20 to 30. Send for your Belt TODAY. Enclose just $1.00 . . . SPACE PATROL BELT arrives Postage Paid.
SPACE BELTS, P.O. BOX 7736
LOS ANGELES 15, CALIFORNIA
MAIL THIS COUPON TODAY..SURE
SPACE BELTS, P.O. BOX 7736
LOS ANGELES 15, CALIFORNIA
Please rush me the following SPACE PATROL BELTS at $1.00 each, POSTAGE PREPAID.
(Check colors) ☐ Black Night
☐ Blasting Red ☐ Jet Green ☐ Ray Tan
Belt size(s) ______ No. of Belts wanted ______
Enclosed find $ ______ Cash (or) $ ______ Check.
No C.O.D.'s.
NAME ______
(Print Clearly)
ADDRESS ______ ZONE ______
CITY ______ STATE ______ SP2

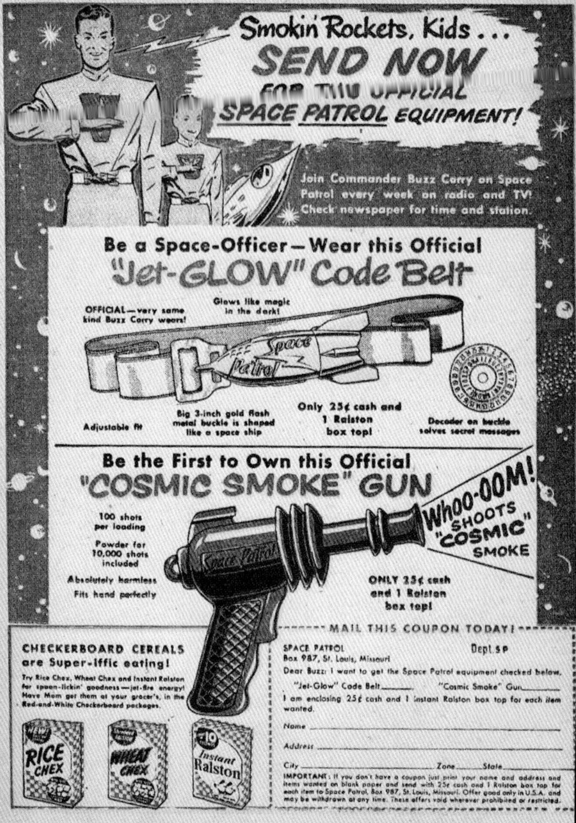
Smokin' Rockets, Kids . . .
SEND NOW
FOR THIS OFFICIAL
SPACE PATROL EQUIPMENT!
Join Commander Buzz Corry on Space Patrol every week on radio and TV! Check newspaper for time and station.
Be a Space-Officer — Wear this Official
"Jet-GLOW" Code Belt
OFFICIAL — very same kind Buzz Corry wears!
Glows like magic in the dark!
Space Patrol
Adjustable fit
Big 3-inch gold flash metal buckle is shaped like a space ship
Only 25¢ cash and 1 Ralston box top!
Decoder on buckle solves secret messages
Be the First to Own this Official
"COSMIC SMOKE" GUN
100 shots per loading
Powder for 10,000 shots included
Absolutely harmless
Fits hand perfectly
Space Patrol
Whoo-OOM! SHOOTS "COSMIC" SMOKE
ONLY 25¢ cash and 1 Ralston box top!
CHECKERBOARD CEREALS are Super-iffic eating!
Try Rice Chex, Wheat Chex and Instant Ralston for spoon-lickin' goodness — jet-fire energy! Have Mom get them at your grocer's, in the Red-and-White Checkerboard packages.
RICE CHEX
WHEAT CHEX
Instant Ralston
MAIL THIS COUPON TODAY!
SPACE PATROL
Box 987, St. Louis, Missouri
Dept. SP
Dear Buzz: I want to get the Space Patrol equipment checked below.
"Jet-Glow" Code Belt ____ "Cosmic Smoke" Gun ____
I am enclosing 25¢ cash and 1 Instant Ralston box top for each item wanted.
Name ____
Address ____
City ____ Zone ____ State ____
IMPORTANT: If you don't have a coupon just print your name and address and items wanted on blank paper and send with 25¢ cash and 1 Ralston box top for each item to Space Patrol, Box 987, St. Louis, Missouri. Offer good only in U.S.A. and may be withdrawn at any time. These offers void wherever prohibited or restricted.

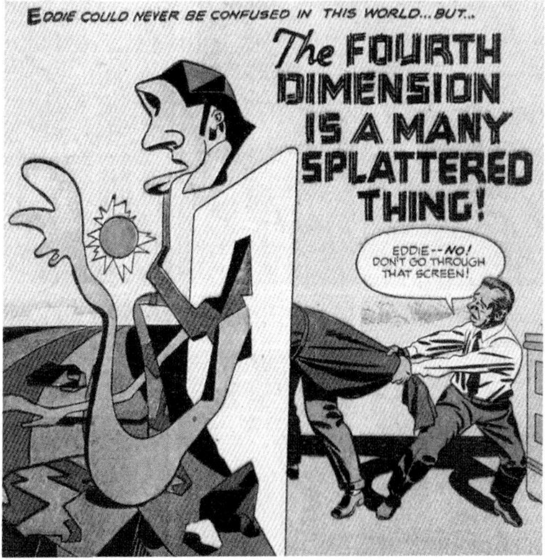
EDDIE COULD NEVER BE CONFUSED IN THIS WORLD... BUT...
The FOURTH DIMENSION IS A MANY SPLATTERED THING!
EDDIE--NO! DON'T GO THROUGH THAT SCREEN!

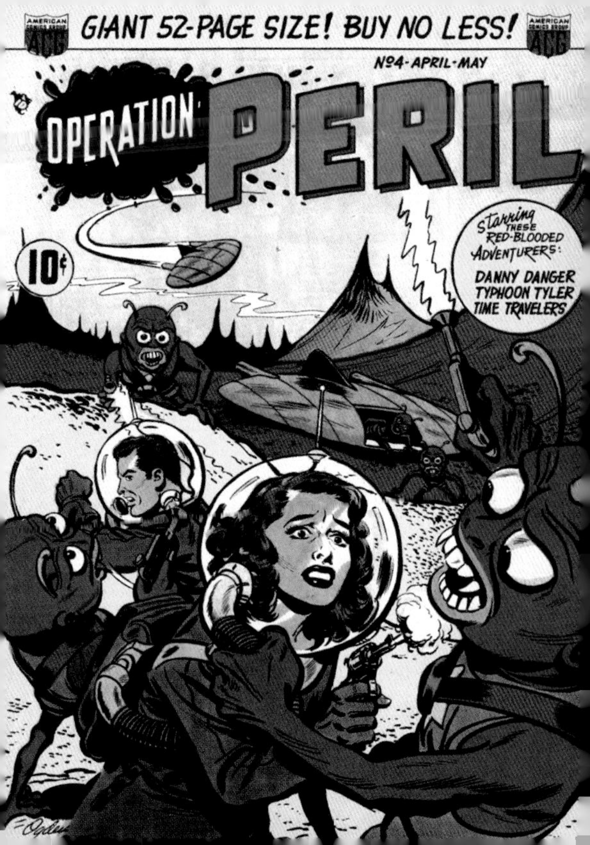
AMERICAN COMICS GROUP ACG
GIANT 52-PAGE SIZE! BUY NO LESS!
AMERICAN COMICS GROUP ACG
Nº4 · APRIL · MAY
OPERATION PERIL
10¢
Starring THESE RED-BLOODED ADVENTURERS:
DANNY DANGER
TYPHOON TYLER
TIME TRAVELERS

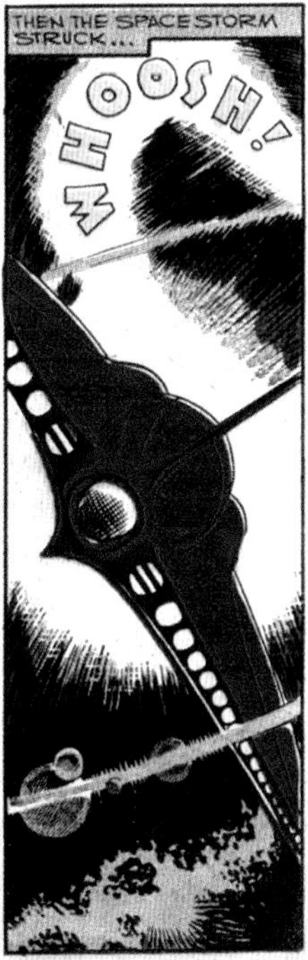
THEN THE SPACE STORM STRUCK...
WHOOSH!

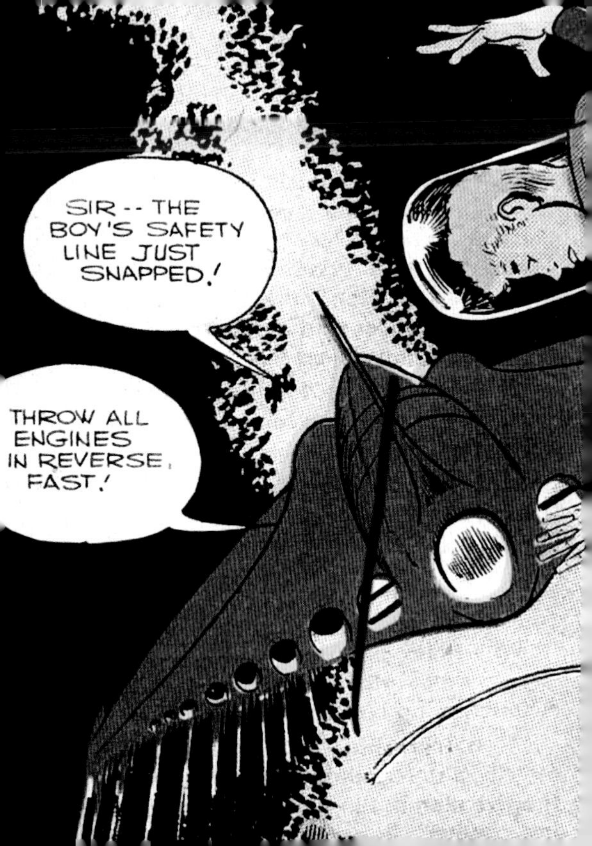
SIR -- THE BOY'S SAFETY LINE JUST SNAPPED!
THROW ALL ENGINES IN REVERSE, FAST!

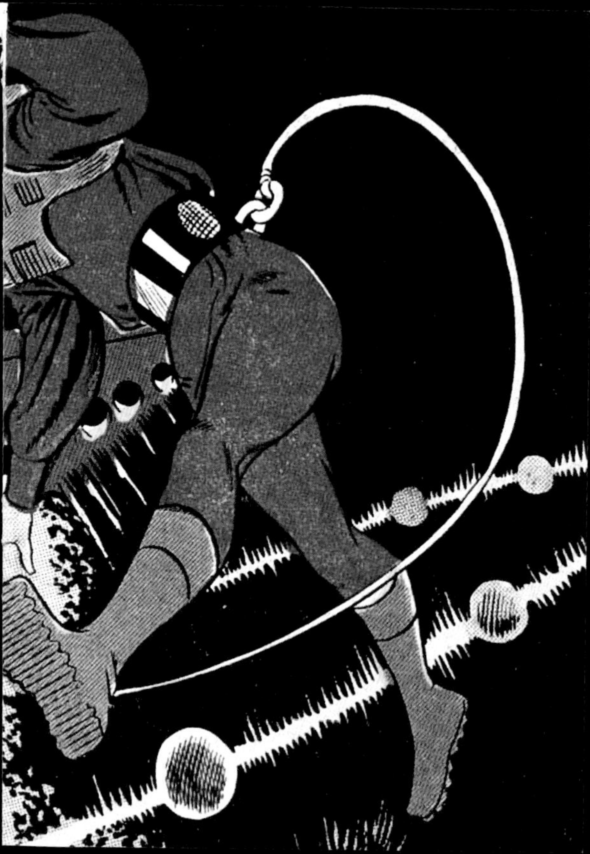

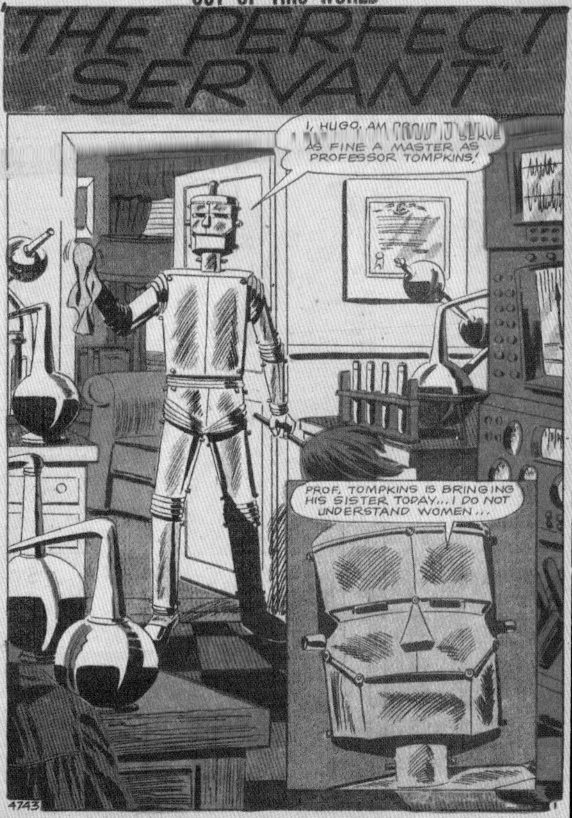
THE PERFECT SERVANT
I, HUGO, AM
AS FINE A MASTER AS PROFESSOR TOMPKINS!
PROF. TOMPKINS IS BRINGING HIS SISTER TODAY... I DO NOT UNDERSTAND WOMEN...
4743

He was just an ordinary guy, doing his job in space! He didn't explore worlds or battle monsters or make the Nine Planet Final with heroic deeds! In fact, you might call his job dull...routine...but you'd be wrong! For a saga of space is born amid thundering meteors when he does his duty as a spaceman and saves...
THE SPACE TREASURE

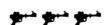

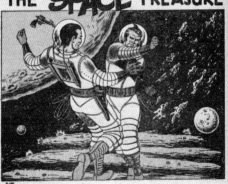

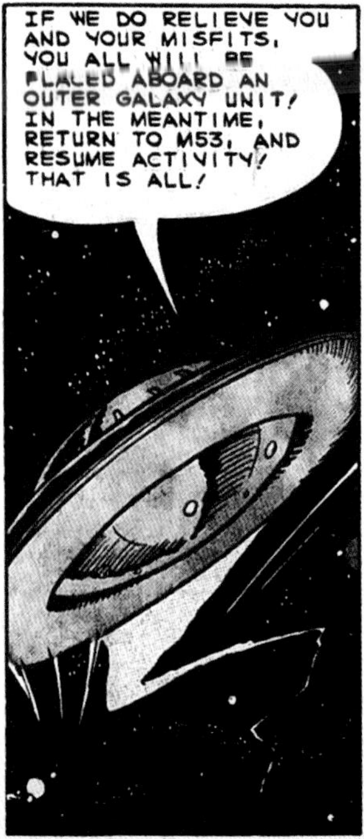
IF WE DO RELIEVE YOU AND YOUR MISFITS, YOU ALL WILL BE PLACED ABOARD AN OUTER GALAXY UNIT! IN THE MEANTIME, RETURN TO M53, AND RESUME ACTIVITY! THAT IS ALL!

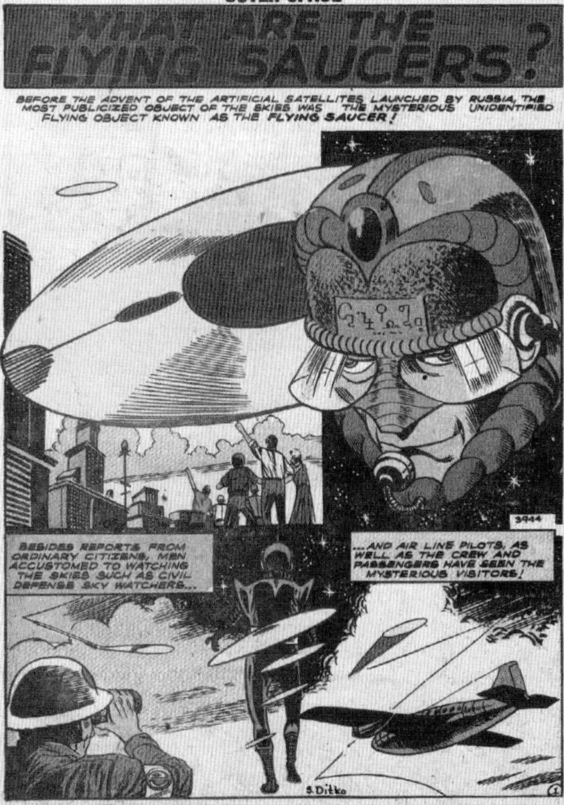
WHAT ARE THE FLYING SAUCERS?
BEFORE THE ADVENT OF THE ARTIFICIAL SATELLITES LAUNCHED BY RUSSIA, THE MOST PUBLICIZED OBJECT OF THE SKIES WAS THE MYSTERIOUS UNIDENTIFIED FLYING OBJECT KNOWN AS THE FLYING SAUCER!
3944
BESIDES REPORTS FROM ORDINARY CITIZENS, MEN ACCUSTOMED TO WATCHING THE SKIES SUCH AS CIVIL DEFENSE SKY WATCHERS...
...AND AIR LINE PILOTS, AS WELL AS THE CREW AND PASSENGERS HAVE SEEN THE MYSTERIOUS VISITORS!
S. Ditko

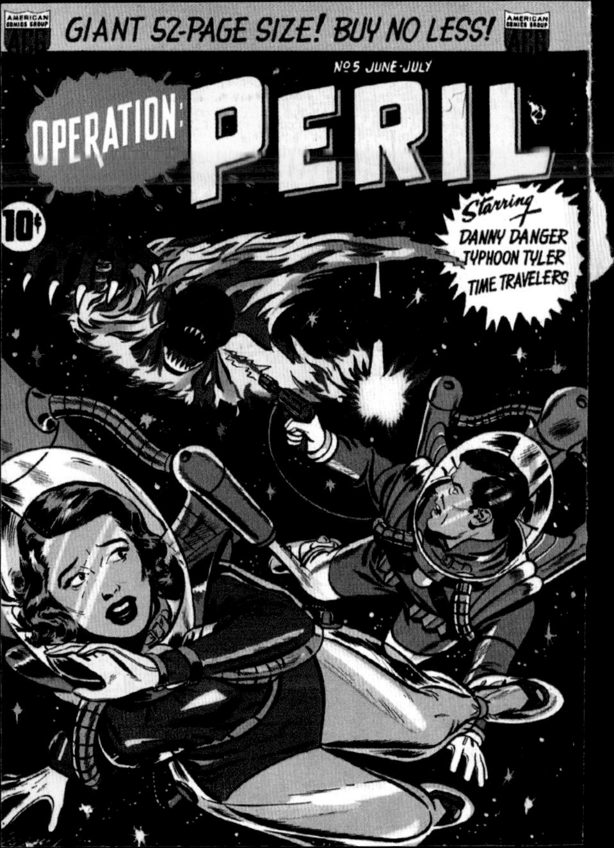

AMERICAN COMICS GROUP
GIANT 52-PAGE SIZE! BUY NO LESS!
AMERICAN COMICS GROUP
No 5 JUNE-JULY
OPERATION: PERIL
10¢
Starring
DANNY DANGER
TYPHOON TYLER
TIME TRAVELERS

HE SAID THE WOMAN LIKE TO SEE ON THE TABLE...
I HAVE MADE THE WINDOWS CLEAN SO THEY GLEAM LIKE JEWELS!

WHO...?
WE ARE FROM A PLANET IN OUTER SPACE, ZION 5!

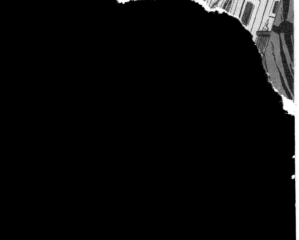

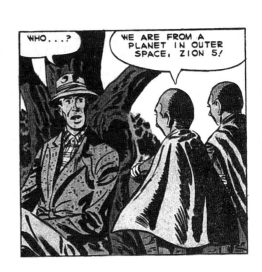

THE BOMB

Dr. Vera Raymond noticed the scientists in the auditorium and scowled. It was the second time that they rejected him. The first occasion was six months ago. Then the [illegible] of Scientists disapproved of his theory as men of science should—in quiet, dignified voting. Now, however, there were howls, catcalls, insults; emotions that penetrated Raymond's very core.

Even then Raymond calculated his revenge. It was his only weapon. His decision was final, even though he had made it in the shadow of a second.

"I'm sorry, Raymond. Very sorry!"

It was Jenkins, Raymond's assistant and friend. He had worked with Raymond on the project and he was the only one who agreed with Raymond on his theory.

"Maybe next time," Jenkins continued.

"No, there will be no next time," Raymond answered.

Jenkins noticed a dangerous semblance of finality in Raymond's voice.

"What do you mean, Dr. Raymond? We'll try again. Sooner or later they have to believe us!"

"There is only one way to deal with that lot of insulting blockheads," he shouted, his voice echoing through the hall. Then, abruptly, he turned from Jenkins and headed for his car.

"Only one way!"

Driving to the Site, Raymond reasoned that the bomb would be relatively easy for him to detonate. He had the ability and the know-how. As Head Controller of the Site, his very presence meant unquestioned authority.

He was in the dread Chamber now, the room that contained all he needed for the bomb. Silently, he applied himself. First he obtained the cone, sliding the cartridge open so that he could inject the explosive. Everything was going smoothly. As he knew, he was experiencing no difficulty. He went to the tomb, carefully sliding open the thick doors, and retrieving the explosive. Carefully, taking extreme caution, aching, creaking deliberation—only he knew, and Jenkins knew, how slow he had to go—he slipped the explosive into the cone.

He breathed easier now.

"Are you insane, Dr. Raymond?"

"Jenkins!" Raymond stared in amazement at his assistant.

"How could you do this, Dr. Raymond?" Jenkins asked.

"You can't stop me, Jenkins!"

"You're wrong," Jenkins said with surety. "I have the guards waiting outside." Then, slowly Jenkins walked towards Raymond, politely but firmly taking him by the arm.

"You're right, Jenkins," Dr. Raymond uttered. "I was beside myself."

"More than that," Jenkins muttered.

"You were hysterical! How could you expect to blow up the Council with a hydrogen bomb?"

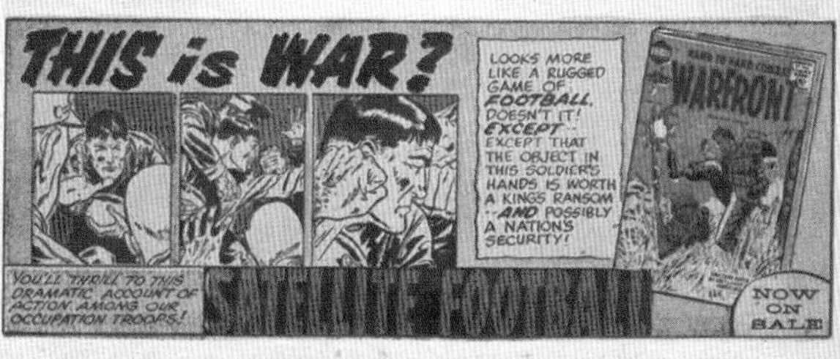

THIS is WAR?
LOOKS MORE LIKE A RUGGED GAME OF FOOTBALL, DOESN'T IT! EXCEPT... EXCEPT THAT THE OBJECT IN THIS SOLDIER'S HANDS IS WORTH A KINGS RANSOM --AND POSSIBLY A NATIONS SECURITY!
WARFRONT
YOU'LL THRILL TO THIS DRAMATIC ACCOUNT OF ACTION AMONG OUR OCCUPATION TROOPS!
NOW ON SALE

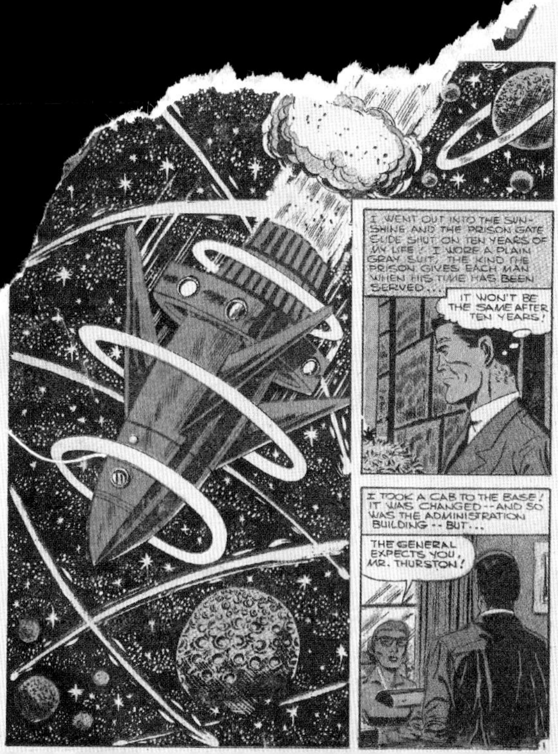
I WENT OUT INTO THE SUN-SHINE AND THE PRISON GATE SLIDE SHUT ON TEN YEARS OF MY LIFE! I WORE A PLAIN GRAY SUIT, THE KIND THE PRISON GIVES EACH MAN WHEN HIS TIME HAS BEEN SERVED...
IT WON'T BE THE SAME AFTER TEN YEARS!
I TOOK A CAB TO THE BASE! IT WAS CHANGED--AND SO WAS THE ADMINISTRATION BUILDING--BUT...
THE GENERAL EXPECTS YOU, MR. THURSTON!

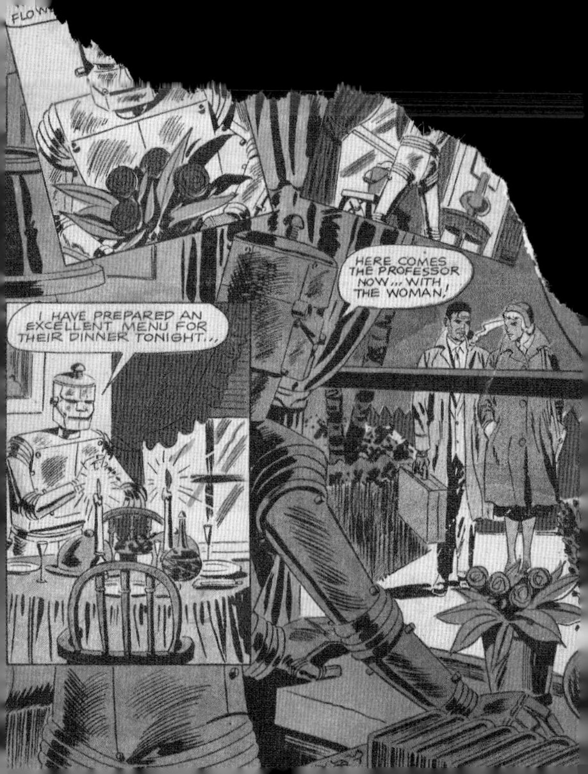
I HAVE PREPARED AN EXCELLENT MENU FOR THEIR DINNER TONIGHT...
HERE COMES THE PROFESSOR NOW... WITH THE WOMAN!

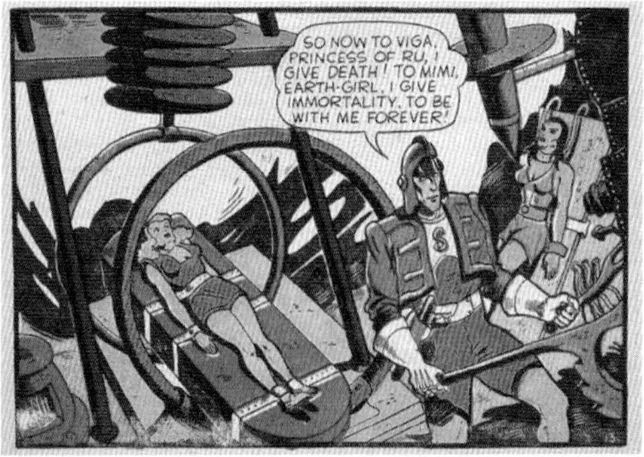
SO NOW TO VIGA, PRINCESS OF RU, I GIVE DEATH! TO MIMI, EARTH-GIRL, I GIVE IMMORTALITY, TO BE WITH ME FOREVER!

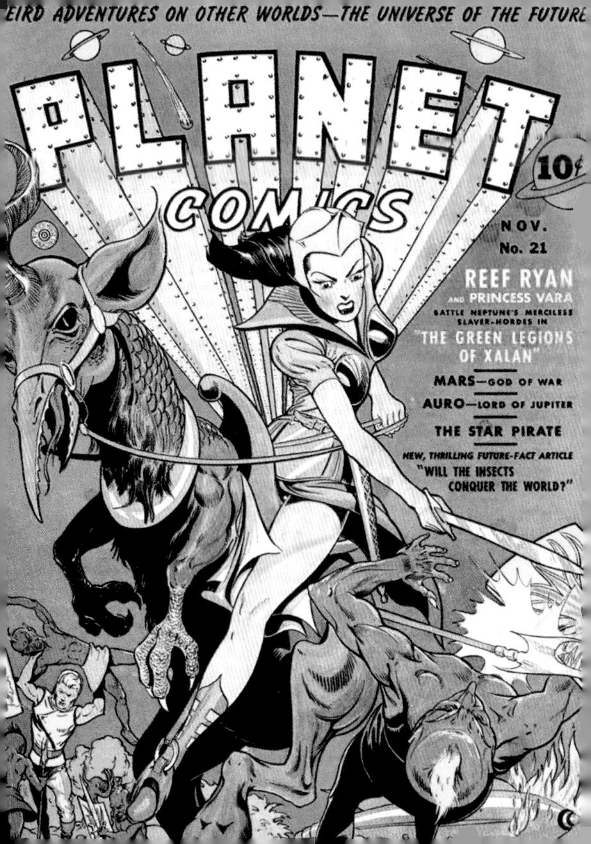

EIRD ADVENTURES ON OTHER WORLDS—THE UNIVERSE OF THE FUTURE
PLANET COMICS
10¢
NOV.
No. 21
REEF RYAN
AND PRINCESS VARA
BATTLE NEPTUNE'S MERCILESS SLAVER-HORDES IN
"THE GREEN LEGIONS OF XALAN"
MARS—GOD OF WAR
AURO—LORD OF JUPITER
THE STAR PIRATE
NEW, THRILLING FUTURE-FACT ARTICLE
"WILL THE INSECTS CONQUER THE WORLD?"

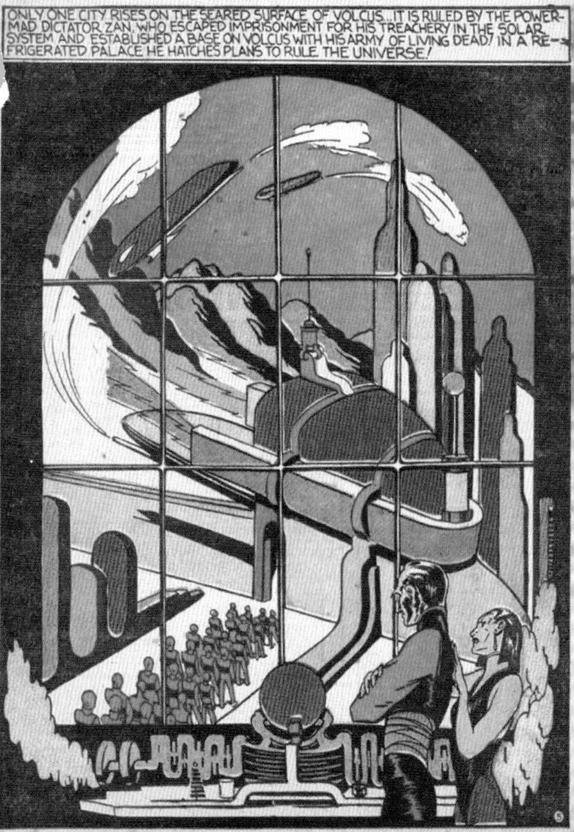
ONLY ONE CITY RISES ON THE SEARED SURFACE OF VOLCUS... IT IS RULED BY THE POWER-MAD DICTATOR ZAN, WHO ESCAPED IMPRISONMENT FOR HIS TREACHERY IN THE SOLAR SYSTEM AND ESTABLISHED A BASE ON VOLCUS WITH HIS ARMY OF LIVING DEAD! IN A REFRIGERATED PALACE HE HATCHES PLANS TO RULE THE UNIVERSE!

The TIME-TRAVELER FOUND STRANGE FRIENDS IN THE WORLD OF THE FUTURE... AND THE CHANCE TO BEAT...

THE LAST ENEMY!

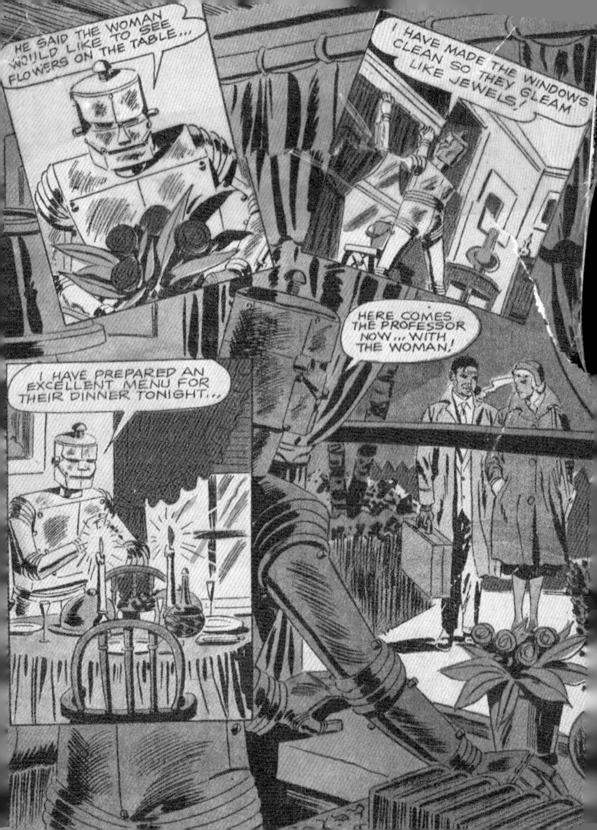
HE SAID THE WOMAN WOULD LIKE TO SEE FLOWERS ON THE TABLE...
I HAVE MADE THE WINDOWS CLEAN SO THEY GLEAM LIKE JEWELS!
I HAVE PREPARED AN EXCELLENT MENU FOR THEIR DINNER TONIGHT...
HERE COMES THE PROFESSOR NOW... WITH THE WOMAN!

OUT OF THIS WORLD

ROCK THURSTON WAS AN ACE WITH AN ENVIABLE RECORD! NO ONE WOULD EVER HAVE SUSPEC ED HIM OF...

DEFECTION

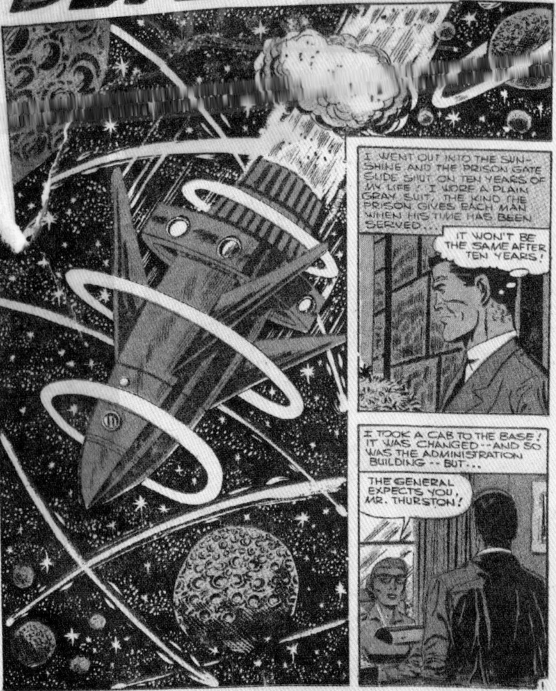
I WENT OUT INTO THE SUN-SHINE AND THE PRISON GATE SLIDE SHUT ON TEN YEARS OF MY LIFE! I WORE A PLAIN GRAY SUIT, THE KIND THE PRISON GIVES EACH MAN WHEN HIS TIME HAS BEEN SERVED...
IT WON'T BE THE SAME AFTER TEN YEARS!
I TOOK A CAB TO THE BASE! IT WAS CHANGED--AND SO WAS THE ADMINISTRATION BUILDING--BUT...
THE GENERAL EXPECTS YOU, MR. THURSTON!

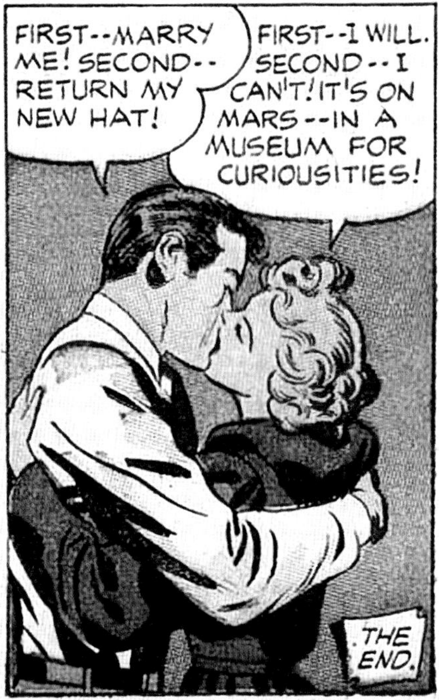
FIRST--MARRY ME! SECOND-- RETURN MY NEW HAT!
FIRST--I WILL. SECOND--I CAN'T! IT'S ON MARS--IN A MUSEUM FOR CURIOUSITIES!
THE END.

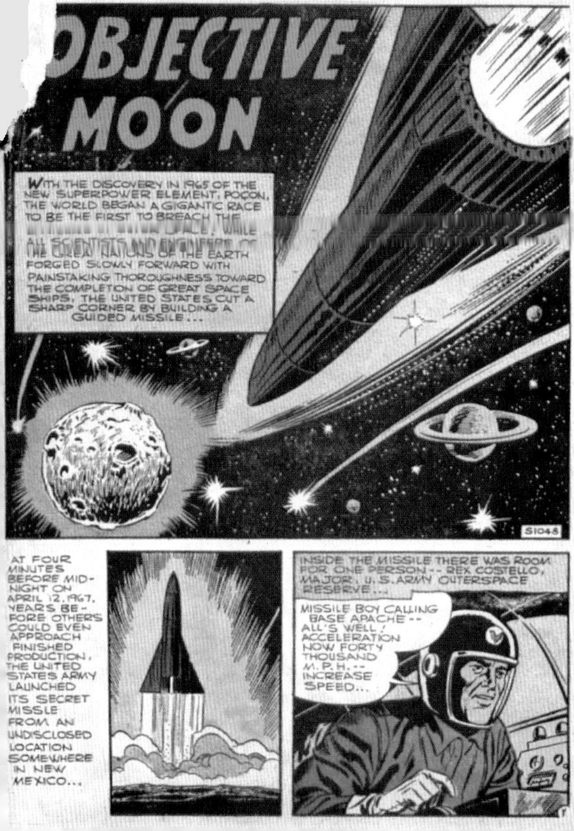
OBJECTIVE MOON
WITH THE DISCOVERY IN 1965 OF THE NEW SUPERPOWER ELEMENT, POÇON, THE WORLD BEGAN A GIGANTIC RACE TO BE THE FIRST TO BREACH THE
WHILE
ALL SCIENTISTS AND ENGINEERS OF THE GREAT NATIONS OF THE EARTH FORGED SLOWLY FORWARD WITH PAINSTAKING THOROUGHNESS TOWARD THE COMPLETION OF GREAT SPACE SHIPS, THE UNITED STATES CUT A SHARP CORNER BY BUILDING A GUIDED MISSILE...
S1048
AT FOUR MINUTES BEFORE MID-NIGHT ON APRIL 12, 1967, YEARS BE-FORE OTHERS COULD EVEN APPROACH FINISHED PRODUCTION, THE UNITED STATES ARMY LAUNCHED ITS SECRET MISSLE FROM AN UNDISCLOSED LOCATION SOMEWHERE IN NEW MEXICO...
INSIDE THE MISSILE THERE WAS ROOM FOR ONE PERSON -- REX COSTELLO, MAJOR, U.S. ARMY OUTERSPACE RESERVE...
MISSILE BOY CALLING BASE APACHE -- ALL'S WELL! ACCELERATION NOW FORTY THOUSAND M.P.H. -- INCREASE SPEED...

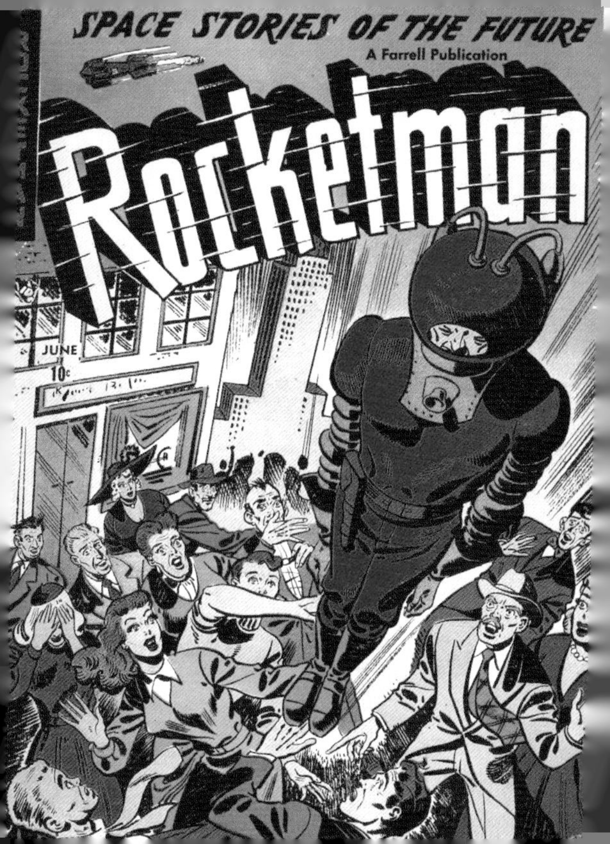
SPACE STORIES OF THE FUTURE
A Farrell Publication
Rocketman
JUNE
10¢

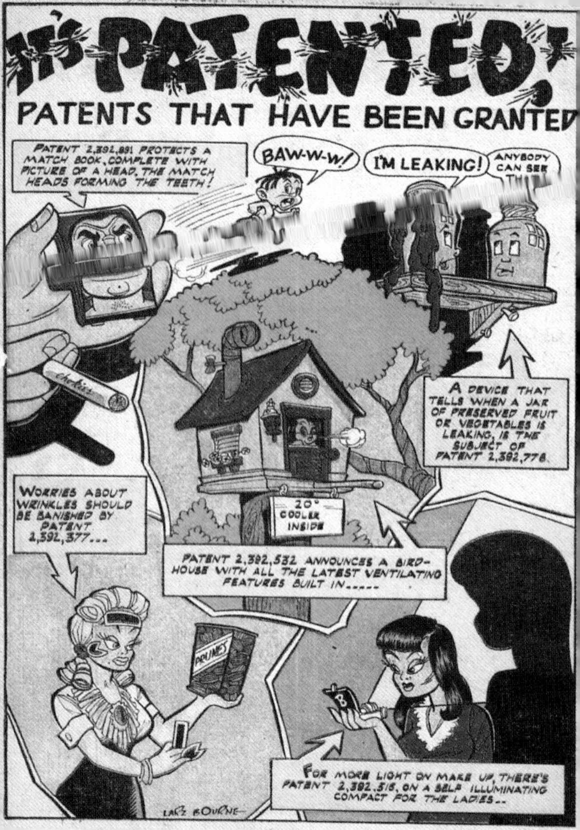
IT'S PATENTED!
PATENTS THAT HAVE BEEN GRANTED
PATENT 2,392,891 PROTECTS A MATCH BOOK, COMPLETE WITH PICTURE OF A HEAD, THE MATCH HEADS FORMING THE TEETH!
BAW-W-W!
I'M LEAKING!
ANYBODY CAN SEE
A DEVICE THAT TELLS WHEN A JAR OF PRESERVED FRUIT OR VEGETABLES IS LEAKING, IS THE SUBJECT OF PATENT 2,392,778
20° COOLER INSIDE
WORRIES ABOUT WRINKLES SHOULD BE BANISHED BY PATENT 2,392,377...
PATENT 2,392,532 ANNOUNCES A BIRD-HOUSE WITH ALL THE LATEST VENTILATING FEATURES BUILT IN.....
PRUNES
FOR MORE LIGHT ON MAKE UP, THERE'S PATENT 2,392,516, ON A SELF ILLUMINATING COMPACT FOR THE LADIES..
LARZ BOURNE

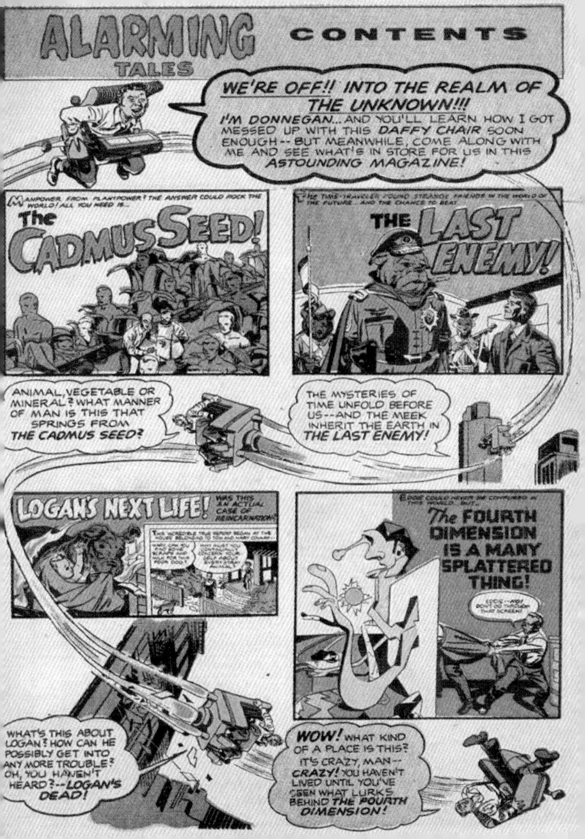
ALARMING TALES
CONTENTS
WE'RE OFF!! INTO THE REALM OF THE UNKNOWN!!!
I'M DONNEGAN... AND YOU'LL LEARN HOW I GOT MESSED UP WITH THIS DAFFY CHAIR SOON ENOUGH -- BUT MEANWHILE, COME ALONG WITH ME AND SEE WHAT'S IN STORE FOR US IN THIS ASTOUNDING MAGAZINE!
MANPOWER FROM PLANTPOWER? THE ANSWER COULD ROCK THE WORLD! ALL YOU NEED IS...
The CADMUS SEED!
THE TIME-TRAVELER FOUND STRANGE FRIENDS IN THE WORLD OF THE FUTURE... AND THE CHANCE TO BEAT
THE LAST ENEMY!
ANIMAL, VEGETABLE OR MINERAL? WHAT MANNER OF MAN IS THIS THAT SPRINGS FROM THE CADMUS SEED?
THE MYSTERIES OF TIME UNFOLD BEFORE US--AND THE MEEK INHERIT THE EARTH IN THE LAST ENEMY!
LOGAN'S NEXT LIFE!
WAS THIS AN ACTUAL CASE OF REINCARNATION?
The FOURTH DIMENSION IS A MANY SPLATTERED THING!
WHAT'S THIS ABOUT LOGAN? HOW CAN HE POSSIBLY GET INTO ANY MORE TROUBLE? OH, YOU HAVEN'T HEARD?--LOGAN'S DEAD!
WOW! WHAT KIND OF A PLACE IS THIS? IT'S CRAZY, MAN--CRAZY! YOU HAVEN'T LIVED UNTIL YOU'VE SEEN WHAT LURKS BEHIND THE FOURTH DIMENSION!

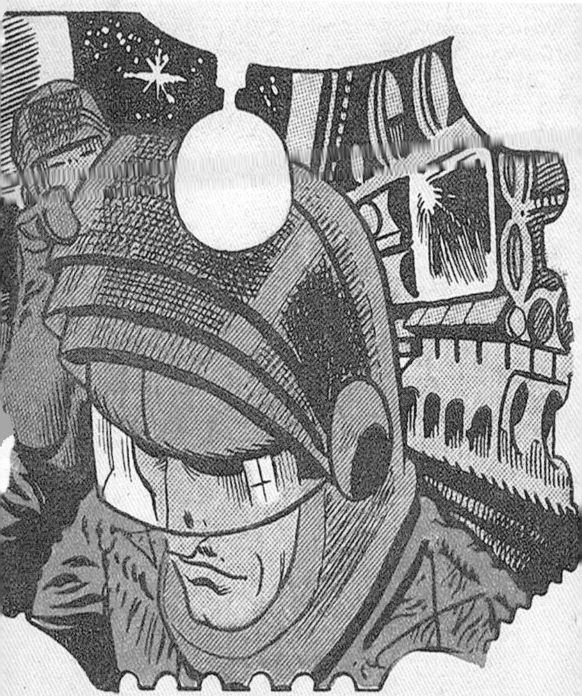

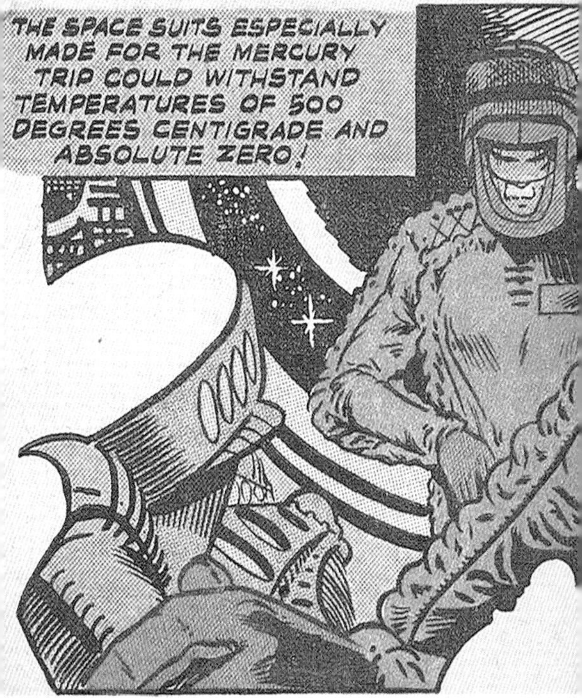
THE SPACE SUITS ESPECIALLY MADE FOR THE MERCURY TRIP COULD WITHSTAND TEMPERATURES OF 500 DEGREES CENTIGRADE AND ABSOLUTE ZERO!

MAN ALONE

Since he was a little child, he had known that he was different. He could do things other children couldn't do and they feared him and so he had been a lonely child. He had learned even to hide the powers he possessed, but in secret he had tried them and developed them, those latent powers. As he grew into manhood, he could evaluate how different he really was. Now in the University, he had to control the quickness of his mentality and [illegible] to be ordinary.

He knew now what he was—a human mutation, having strange powers never given to man before. And he was lonelier than ever for a man like him could have no friends, no romance, no closeness with another person or they might learn his secret, shun him, and make him an outcast.

It was on his twenty-first birthday that he first became aware of the others, the ones who lurked in the shadows and followed him, the strange, mental tentacles that probed at his mind when he was relaxed in sleep and caused him to awaken with a scream in his throat. Who were they? What were they? What did they want of him? That they were alien, not like the people he was familiar with, this he knew.

The loneliness, mounting these last few years, throttling all the natural desires of a young man, the knowledge of his difference from others, combined with this new probing and following brought fear. He must run, hide . . . but where? Was there any place in the world where he would be welcome? He knew there wasn't!

He climbed the stairs to his lonely room. He would pack this night and flee. He would keep going, away from the alien beings who had discovered him. He entered his darkened room, and immediately sensed the presence of others. The door slammed behind him as he turned to run. A switch clicked and the room was flooded with light. A girl and a man were there. He remembered the girl, [illegible] had seen her before and had wistfully thought how lovely she was and how he would like to meet her. She smiled at him now and spoke:

"We know your problems! We've been watching you, probing at your mind, with thought beams! We knew all about you!"

"Then . . . then what am I? And what do you want of me?"

The man answered, "You are a mutation, the next step in the evolution of mankind! There are others like you. Carol here, is one of you. We are searching the world and finding all of you, training you in a hidden valley to extend your powers for you are the hope of mankind and the future!"

The girl took his arm. "Come, you must join us in the valley!"

He looked into her eyes, and in that moment a feeling of contentment such as he had never known flooded him and he knew he would never be lonely again.

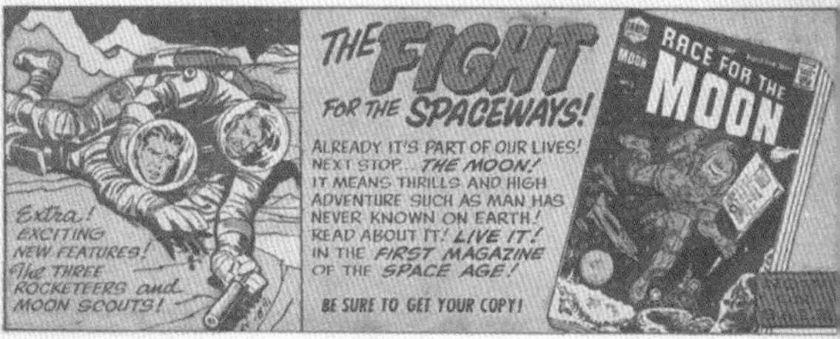

THE FIGHT FOR THE SPACEWAYS!
ALREADY IT'S PART OF OUR LIVES! NEXT STOP... THE MOON! IT MEANS THRILLS AND HIGH ADVENTURE SUCH AS MAN HAS NEVER KNOWN ON EARTH! READ ABOUT IT! LIVE IT! IN THE FIRST MAGAZINE OF THE SPACE AGE!
BE SURE TO GET YOUR COPY!
Extra! EXCITING NEW FEATURES! The THREE ROCKETEERS and MOON SCOUTS!
RACE FOR THE MOON

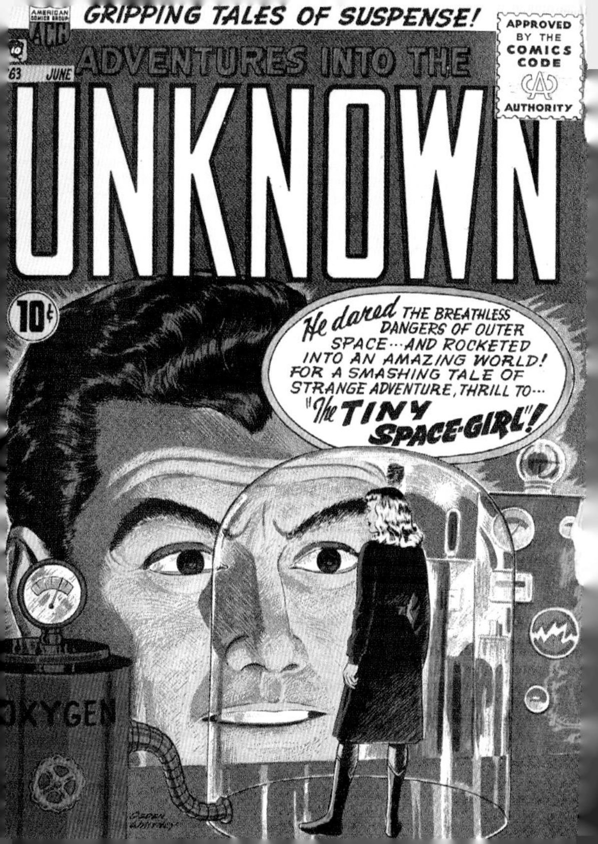
AMERICAN COMICS GROUP
ACG
GRIPPING TALES OF SUSPENSE!
APPROVED BY THE COMICS CODE AUTHORITY
63 JUNE
ADVENTURES INTO THE
UNKNOWN
10¢
He dared THE BREATHLESS DANGERS OF OUTER SPACE···AND ROCKETED INTO AN AMAZING WORLD! FOR A SMASHING TALE OF STRANGE ADVENTURE, THRILL TO··· "The TINY SPACE-GIRL"!
OXYGEN

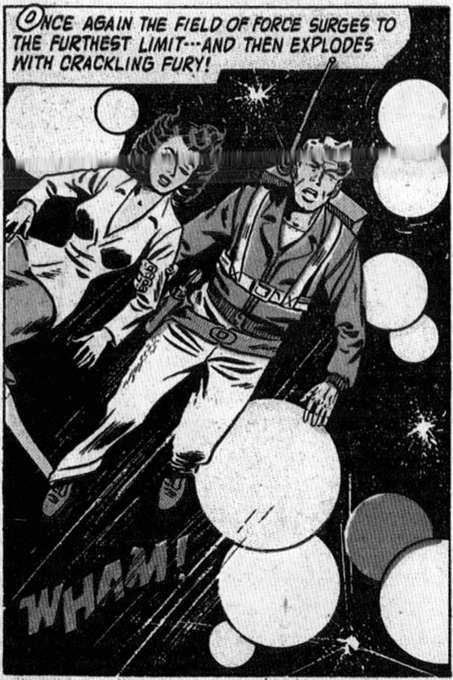
ONCE AGAIN THE FIELD OF FORCE SURGES TO THE FURTHEST LIMIT---AND THEN EXPLODES WITH CRACKLING FURY!
WHAM!

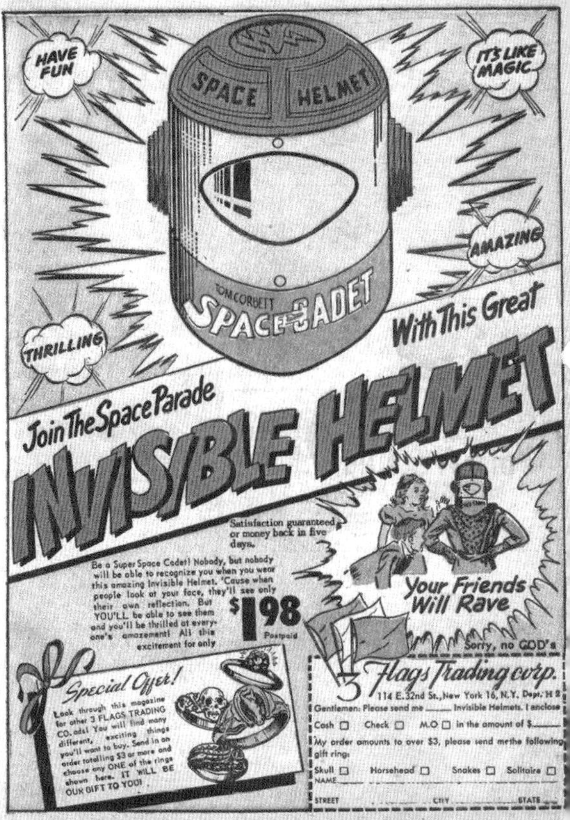

HAVE FUN
IT'S LIKE MAGIC
SPACE HELMET
AMAZING
THRILLING
TOM CORBETT SPACE CADET
Join The Space Parade With This Great
INVISIBLE HELMET
Satisfaction guaranteed or money back in five days.
Be a Super Space Cadet! Nobody, but nobody will be able to recognize you when you wear this amazing Invisible Helmet. 'Cause when people look at your face, they'll see only their own reflection. But YOU'LL be able to see them and you'll be thrilled at every-one's amazement! All this excitement for only
$198 Postpaid
Your Friends Will Rave
Sorry, no C.O.D.'s
Special Offer!
Look through this magazine for other 3 FLAGS TRADING CO. ads! You will find many different, exciting things you'll want to buy. Send in an order totalling $3 or more and choose any ONE of the rings shown here. IT WILL BE OUR GIFT TO YOU!
3 Flags Trading corp.
114 E. 32nd St., New York 16, N.Y. Dept. H 2
Gentlemen: Please send me ____ Invisible Helmets. I enclose
Cash ☐ Check ☐ M.O ☐ in the amount of $____
My order amounts to over $3, please send me the following gift ring:
Skull ☐ Horsehead ☐ Snakes ☐ Solitaire ☐
NAME
STREET CITY STATE

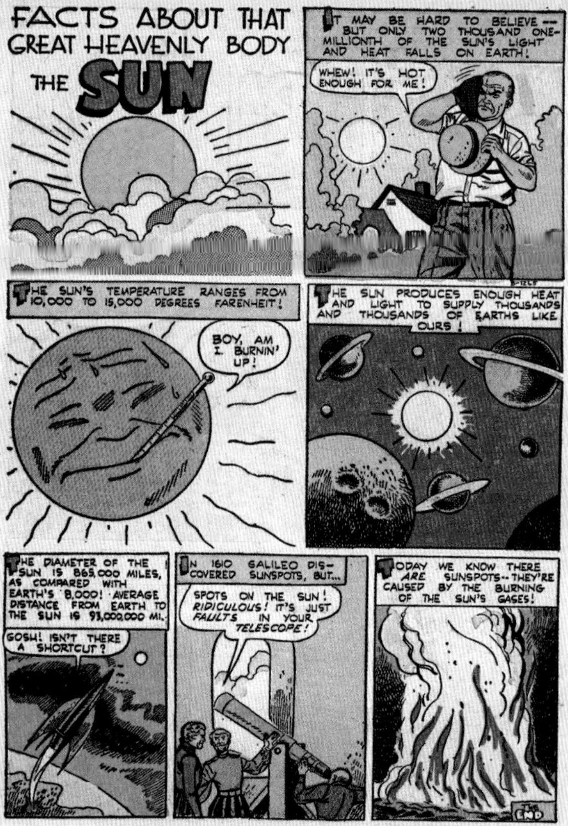
FACTS ABOUT THAT GREAT HEAVENLY BODY THE SUN
IT MAY BE HARD TO BELIEVE -- BUT ONLY TWO THOUSAND ONE-MILLIONTH OF THE SUN'S LIGHT AND HEAT FALLS ON EARTH!
WHEW! IT'S HOT ENOUGH FOR ME!
THE SUN'S TEMPERATURE RANGES FROM 10,000 TO 15,000 DEGREES FARENHEIT!
BOY, AM I BURNIN' UP!
THE SUN PRODUCES ENOUGH HEAT AND LIGHT TO SUPPLY THOUSANDS AND THOUSANDS OF EARTHS LIKE OURS!
THE DIAMETER OF THE SUN IS 865,000 MILES, AS COMPARED WITH EARTH'S 8,000! AVERAGE DISTANCE FROM EARTH TO THE SUN IS 93,000,000 MI.
GOSH! ISN'T THERE A SHORTCUT?
IN 1610 GALILEO DISCOVERED SUNSPOTS, BUT...
SPOTS ON THE SUN! RIDICULOUS! IT'S JUST FAULTS IN YOUR TELESCOPE!
TODAY WE KNOW THERE ARE SUNSPOTS -- THEY'RE CAUSED BY THE BURNING OF THE SUN'S GASES!
THE END

THE BOMB

Dr. Vera Raymond noticed the scientists in the auditorium and scowled. It was the second time that they rejected him. The first occasion was six months ago. Then this Council of Scientists disapproved of his theory as men of science should—in quiet, dignified voting. Now, however, there were howls, catcalls, insults; emotions that penetrated Raymond's very core.

Even then Raymond calculated his revenge. It was his only weapon. His decision was final, even though he had made it in the shadow of a second.

"I'm sorry, Raymond. Very sorry!"

It was Jenkins, Raymond's assistant and friend. He had worked with Raymond on the project and he was the only one who agreed with Raymond on his theory.

"Maybe next time," Jenkins continued.

"No, there will be no next time," Raymond answered.

Jenkins noticed a dangerous semblance of finality in Raymond's voice.

"What do you mean, Dr. Raymond? We'll try again. Sooner or later they have to believe us!"

"There is only one way to deal with that lot of insulting blockheads," he shouted, his voice echoing through the hall. Then, abruptly, he turned from Jenkins and headed for his car.

"Only one way!"

Driving to the Site, Raymond reasoned that the bomb would be relatively easy for him to detonate. He had the ability and the know-how. As Head Controller of the Site, his very presence meant unquestioned authority.

He was in the dread Chamber now, the room that contained all he needed for the bomb. Silently, he applied himself. First he obtained the cone, sliding the cartridge open so that he could inject the explosive. Everything was going smoothly. As he knew, he was experiencing no difficulty. He went to the tomb, carefully sliding open the thick doors, and retrieving the explosive. Carefully, taking extreme caution, aching, creaking deliberation—only he knew, and Jenkins knew, how slow he had to go—he slipped the explosive into the cone.

He breathed easier now.

"Are you insane, Dr. Raymond?"

"Jenkins!" Raymond stared in amazement at his assistant.

"How could you do this, Dr. Raymond?" Jenkins asked.

"You can't stop me, Jenkins!"

"You're wrong," Jenkins said with surety. "I have the guards waiting outside." Then, slowly Jenkins walked towards Raymond, politely but firmly taking him by the arm.

"You're right, Jenkins," Dr. Raymond uttered. "I was beside myself."

"More than that," Jenkins muttered.

"You were hysterical! How could you expect to blow up the Council with a hydrogen bomb?"

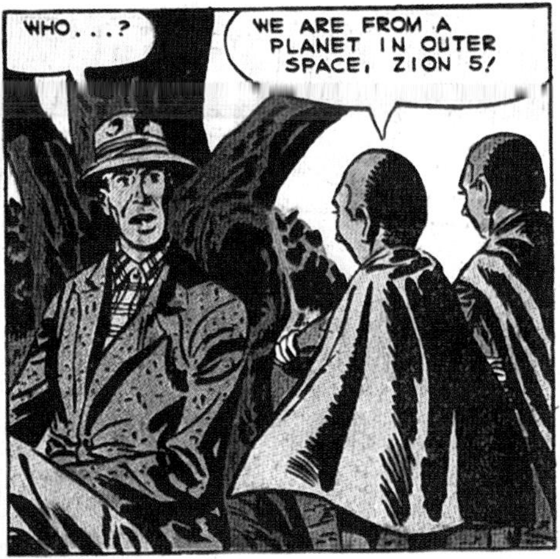
WHO...?
WE ARE FROM A PLANET IN OUTER SPACE, ZION 5!

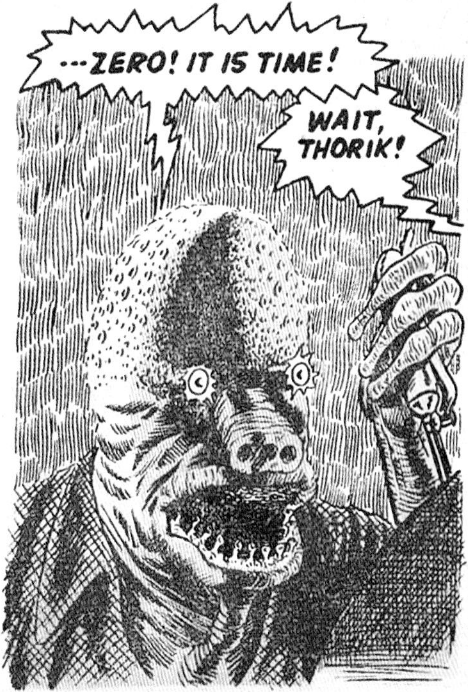
---ZERO! IT IS TIME!
WAIT, THORIK!

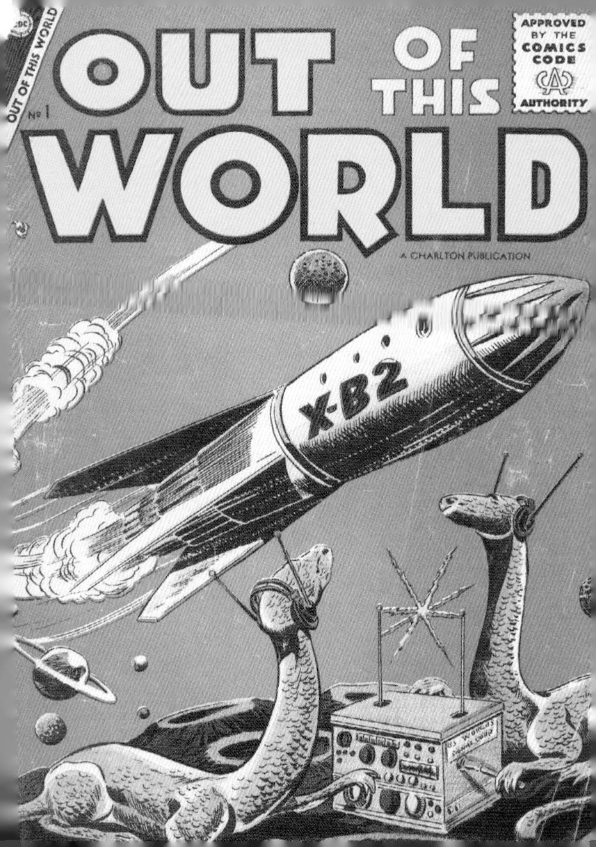
CDC
OUT OF THIS WORLD
No 1
OUT OF THIS WORLD
APPROVED BY THE COMICS CODE AUTHORITY
A CHARLTON PUBLICATION
X-B2